MIGRANT AND SEASONAL AGRICULTURAL WORKERS: PROTECTIVE STATUTES

MIGRANT AND SEASONAL AGRICULTURAL WORKERS: PROTECTIVE STATUTES

WILLIAM G. WHITTAKER

Novinka Books
New York

For permission to use material from this book please contact us:
Telephone 631-231-7269; Fax 631-231-8175
Web Site: http://www.novapublishers.com

NOTICE TO THE READER

LIBRARY OF CONGRESS CATALOGING-IN-PUBLICATION DATA
Available upon request

Available Upon Request
ISBN 978-1-60456-814-1

Published by Nova Science Publishers, Inc. ✦ *New York*

CONTENTS

Preface   **vii**

Chapter 1   Introduction   **1**

Chapter 2   The Farm Labor Contractor Registration Act,
                 Origins, and Congressional Enactment (1964)   **3**

Chapter 3   The First Years of the Farm Labor Contractor
                 Registration Act (1964-1974)   **19**

Chapter 4   Implementing a Revised Statute (1974-1983)   **39**

Chapter 5   A New Statute Emerges (1983 FF.)   **63**

Chapter 6   Agricultural Workers in the New Century   **71**

References   **73**

Index   **91**

PREFACE

Workers in agriculture, generally, have experienced a different pattern of labor-management relations and labor standards from those in the industrial workforce. In part, such disparity was related to the nature of the work and the characteristics of the workers. Some agricultural workers have tended to be migratory or seasonal. They have tended to be employed, more or less casually, for short periods by any single employer who, perhaps not surprisingly, did not want to be burdened by a regular employer-employee relationship. Some agricultural workers are skilled; the majority are probably marginally skilled or unskilled, though they perform necessary services.

Two pieces of legislation, sequentially, have dealt in a significant manner with migrant or seasonal agricultural labor. In 1964, Congress passed the Farm Labor Contractor Registration Act (FLCRA). For a decade, little attention was paid to the statute, but then, in 1974, it was amended, and suddenly, a storm of protest was heard. It was argued that the wrong people were being forced to register. Through the next nine years, various interests sought modification of the act to conform to their perceptions of the original intent of the Congress. In 1983, Congress repealed the FLCRA and replaced it with the Migrant and Seasonal Agricultural Workers' Protection Act (MSPA). With a very few exceptions, MSPA has operated without controversy. But, at the same time, some may ask, has the new enactment been effective?

The two statutes — FLCRA and MSPA — are intimately connected and have triggered similar reactions with respect to immigration policy, to the inability of agricultural workers to organize and to bargain collectively, and to more general labor standards. Some have suggested that practices under FLCRA and of MSPA have been unduly burdensome. Has the concept of *farm labor contractor* been defined with sufficient care? Have agricultural interests made effective use of their employees, providing them with training and with consistency of employment? Might better utilization of employees prove more productive and more profitable? And, might these changes, in turn, prove more attractive to domestic American workers?

This report is a summary and a survey, spelling out the considerations that Congress found were a part of the realities of agricultural employment in 20th (and 21st) Century America. It begins in the 1960s with the advent of FLCRA, and proceeds through the enactment of MSPA and to the end of the century. But, it is also a summary of developments in the history of the two statutes, written from the perspective of a labor economist. It may, from time to time, be revised as new developments occur.

Thus far, in the 110th Congress, no new legislation has been considered that would amend MSPA.

Chapter 1

INTRODUCTION[*]

During the late 1950s, a general congressional interest had developed in the condition of migratory or seasonal farm workers in the United States. Several exploratory hearings had been held, but no new legislation had been adopted. Then, on a Friday evening, the day after Thanksgiving (1960), a television program aired: *Harvest of Shame*, with Edward R. Murrow.

> *Harvest of Shame* was a report on the plight of the migratory farm workers ... who as virtual peons kept the nation's larders stocked. The public reaction to it was one of surprised horror at the conditions portrayed. Farm organizations were horrified for other reasons, charging 'highly colored propaganda' and 'deceit.' Farmers' spokesmen demanded 'equal time'....[1]

The Murrow broadcast emphasized the risks and hazards associated with crew leaders and agricultural employment at large. Whatever the flaws of the film, it provided a context for various pieces of migrant and seasonal farmworker legislation that had been (and would continue to be) before the Congress.

Through the next several years, Congress would consider a number of pieces of remedial legislation focusing upon the farm environment. Two bills that became law are of special importance: the Farm Labor Contractor Registration Act (FLCRA: 1964-1983) and a successor statute, the Migrant and Seasonal Agricultural Workers' Protection Act (MSPA: 1983 ff.). The two statutes, sequentially, provide the basis for regulation of migrant

---

[*] This report is excerpted from CRS Report RL33372, Upated August 29, 2007

agricultural and seasonal agricultural workers. A focal point of each of the statutes, however, has been the farm labor contractor.

Through nearly 50 years, intermittently, the Congress has debated the two statutes and their implications — for labor supply, for immigration, and for equity for the several parties involved. The issues have changed little, though their focus may have been altered. Initially (up to 1974), concern was voiced with respect to farm labor contractors and their alleged excesses. Then, after the 1974 amendments to FLCRA, concern moved away from contractors and toward those who used migrant and seasonal workers: essentially, the growers and their agents. In 1983, FLCRA was repealed and replaced with the Migrant and Seasonal Agricultural Workers Protection Act. The latter (MSPA), with few exceptions (notably, the case of *Adams Fruit*; see below), has remained as written. There have been numerous hearings on the act and, likely, more will follow. This report summarizes debate over the acts and, in that context, the evolution of agricultural labor.

Chapter 2

THE FARM LABOR CONTRACTOR REGISTRATION ACT, ORIGINS, AND CONGRESSIONAL ENACTMENT (1964)

The farm labor contractor (or crew leader) "is the bridge between the farm operator and the migrant laborer." Farm operators would go south each year to "meet the crew leader" and arrange for migratory crews. A large majority of migrants belong to crews. In 1960, it was reported, the largest crew numbered 185 workers, the smallest 13 — with the usual size between 45 and 74 members. The crews grew out of "the need of inarticulate people to have someone to speak for them" and the farmer's problem "of recruiting and handling labor."[2]

In 1959, Senator Harrison Williams (D-NJ) introduced legislation seeking, through federal registration, "to eliminate the relatively few migrant labor contractors who are dishonest and immoral, and who exploit migrant workers and growers." A slightly different bill was introduced by Senators Jacob Javits (R-NY) and Kenneth Keating (R-NY). In the House, Representative James Roosevelt (D-CA) was an early sponsor of such legislation.[3] None of these early bills were approved. It would take hearings and subsequent refinement through three Congresses before their adoption.

THE VARIOUS ROLES
OF THE FARM LABOR CONTRACTOR

In theory, the crew leader is an "independent businessman" with varied tasks. Some crew leaders do little more than recruit for farm operators — but for a farmer several hundred (or several thousand) miles away from the areas of labor supply, that task is monumental. Others become more deeply involved in the management of the crew. The report to the Senate Subcommittee on Migratory Labor (1960) observed that:

Some ... provide transportation for the migrant. Others oversee the work of the crew upon its arrival; manage the camps where the migrants are housed; provide the commissary and food facilities; pay the crew members; haul the produce from the fields to the packing sheds....

The profit for the farm labor contractor "lies in the differential between what they are paid by the farmer and [what they] pay to the worker." Some crew leaders work on a commission basis, taking a few cents from each item produced by crew members.[4]

The list of alleged abuses associated with the farm labor contractor appears to have been as long and varied as those engaged in the field. As the 1961 hearings commenced, William Batt, Pennsylvania's Secretary of Labor and Industry, noted:

"The good ones [crew leaders] say to me, 'I preach to the men to save their money.'" Of the less desirable crew leaders, Batt noted the then standard complaints:

"Changing wage rates without explanation."
"Exploitation of child labor."
"Illegal sale of alcoholic beverages."
"Charging the workers a rental fee on housing provided free by the grower."
"Importation of prostitutes, with sharing of the 'take.'"
"Food profiteering in crew-leader-operated commissaries."
"Hunting deer out of season."
"Shooting and beating up other crew leaders."
"Rigged crew-leader-operated gambling games."
"Paying crew members in 'scrip' in lieu of cash."
"Charging exorbitant transportation fees."

Batt continued. "In the case of one crew leader who kept accurate wage records, the services of a prostitute were a payroll deductible item."[5]

Matt Triggs, speaking for the American Farm Bureau Federation and defending the contractors, suggested that stories of abuse were "told and retold" with a "misleading implication that there is more of this than there really is."[6] Another witness, with legislation in mind, argued that contractors "are educationally unequipped to perform the laborious clerical function this bill would impose."[7] A third stated that with their "limited education," the contractors would be "unable to fill out the necessary forms" that the act will require.[8] Yet another declared "They are not schooled.... Much recordkeeping, much bookkeeping is anathema to them. They are not trained for it."[9] Triggs asserted that "most leaders have previously been migratory workers. They are semi-literate."[10] And, Triggs affirmed, "You have got to realize that an awful lot of these crew leaders are very simple people...."[11]

Nonetheless, contractors may undertake relatively sophisticated responsibilities. Secretary of Labor Willard Wirtz pointed out that, in Oregon, it was "the general practice" of using the crew leader "as a paymaster."[12] The "crew leader acts as an intermediary between the grower and the workers," and in nearly "two thirds (63 percent) of the areas surveyed" nationally, the "workers were paid by the crew leaders...."[13] Similarly, "the crew leader is responsible in certain circumstances for making the necessary deductions and keeping payroll records" with respect to social security participation.[14] Sarah Newman, then of the National Consumers League, observed, "Because crew leaders are under no regulated responsibility to anyone, their many abuses have been able to flourish."[15]

ISSUES IN THE EARLY DEBATE

During three Congresses (from 1959 to 1964), numerous bills (not always labor-related) were introduced to ameliorate the conditions of agricultural workers. As these bills evolved, it was difficult to keep their implications separate. The following section analyses, in a general way, deal with issues and concepts common to many of these proposals.

State Versus Federal

"We do not believe this bill would serve any useful purpose since most farm labor contractors are already registered with one or more State employment services," stated Charles Creuziger, spokesperson for the Vegetable Growers Association of America. "We believe, as a matter of principle, that regulation of the contractors can best be handled by the States."[16]

Industry and non-industry forces divided on the issue of federalism. J. Banks Young of the National Cotton Council urged that the issue was strictly local and that federal intervention "would adversely restrict the availability and mobility of such workers and unnecessarily increase farm costs."[17] Noting the alleged abuses under the current system, Richard O'Connell of the National Council of Farmer Cooperatives stressed the local character of the problem. Most states, he suggested, have "laws prohibiting gambling, prostitution, unlawful narcotics, and liquor sales." If so, "the crew leaders should be indicted under the appropriate laws" and, having "paid their debt," should not be harassed.[18] Triggs also thought local government could handle the issue. "Even if the 9 or 10 farm labor bills now before the Congress were to be enacted, we believe they would represent an ineffectual approach to the problem, and in some cases would be decidedly harmful to the interests of workers and farmers."[19]

Observing that the states already had regulations dealing with labor camps, Triggs stated that "... only a handful of these laws are really adequate." Crew leaders "can evade their regulations by ... going to other States with their crews that do not have licensing requirements." If the federal government were to act, it should focus on "the licensing of crew leaders or contractors of migratory labor."[20]

The problem "requires the leadership of the Federal Government," Secretary Wirtz advised, because of the movement of contractors across state lines. A person "... involved in malpractice in this area is simply likely not to be there when somebody charges him."[21] Others concurred. "A fellow who is fined or barred in one State will simply duck into another State and there perhaps commit the same practices," suggested Arnold Mayer of the Amalgamated Meat Cutters and Butcher Workmen of North America. "The migrant labor stream is an interstate stream and dealing with it needs interstate legislation."[22]

Authority for the Secretary

Industry spokespersons questioned the wisdom of granting new authority to the Secretary of Labor to manage agricultural labor supply. "Many of the terms used ... are not clearly defined," stated Young, of the Cotton Council. As it stands, the "... power to issue regulations under the authority of the bill is extremely broad."[23]

The authority granted to the Secretary, remarked James Moore of the National Apple Institute, would "inevitably result in control by the Secretary ... of the agricultural migratory labor market."[24] The requirement "as to their financial responsibility would impose burdens which few individuals recruiting labor could meet."[25] The proposed legislation would establish the Secretary "as judge, jury, and prosecutor," stated Delmer Robinson of the Frederick County (Virginia) Fruitgrowers Association. "We do not feel that a man's livelihood [the contractor's] should depend on the benevolence of the Secretary of Labor."[26] The Secretary, in accord with his own rules, can put out of business any contractor who has "'failed without justification'" to comply with the regulations — but the proposal "is completely silent as to who would decide whether or not there was 'justification.' It is presumed the Secretary ... could arbitrarily decide this point."[27]

Defining Terms

Through the hearings, concepts to be used in the act were gradually defined. Still, numerous concerns were voiced by industry with respect to the several bills that came before the committees.

Defining a Contractor

The Farm Bureau favored a narrow definition of *contractor* with registration "limited to crew leaders proper, and not extended to all persons who may recruit or transport workers." But how might one distinguish between a labor contractor (to be registered) and *persons who may recruit or transport workers*?[28]

The National Cotton Council argued that the concept of contractor, thus far defined, "would require registration of fraternal, religious, social and other organizations which frequently provide temporary agricultural employment for their members" and processors "who provide workers to farmers."[29] Others argued that the term might include "charitable and religious organizations" and "4-H advisers."[30] The proposal, it was suggested, "seems to make a crew leader out of everyone who contacts more than nine people"[31] and could include groups such as "sugar companies, canneries, and cotton gins" that provide labor only as "incidental to the main services they offer farmers." These, some felt, should be excluded.[32]

Even true crew leaders often work through "responsible employees" who should not have to register. It was argued "... that employees of any registered entity should not be required to register" but, rather, have "a single certificate of registration for the overall recruitment activity...."[33] The definition of contractor, it was urged, "... should be changed to cover the individual ... who gathers a crew of workers in one State and transports them to another State and *stays with them in a supervisory capacity* ... and is the actual crew leader."[34] Again: "We would strongly recommend that you eliminate at least the resident concern, the canner who recruits workers for farmers in the territory, the sugar companies, the cotton gins, ... labor associations, and others that are responsible financially...."[35]

Duration of Registration?

"Registration should be permanent and continue in effect until revoked for cause," the Farm Bureau spokesman held. "We see no valid reason for the annual licensing of crew leaders."[36]

The Department of Labor (DOL), however, *did* recognize a need for annual licensing. "The common phrase, 'fly by night' applies, I suppose, more aptly to this economic situation than to almost any other which I can think of," observed Secretary Wirtz.[37] "All the evidence we have indicates that there is considerable turnover among the crew leader personnel," observed Robert Goodwin of DOL's Bureau of Employment Security, making it "necessary, really, to have an annual certification...." Goodwin took note of auto and other insurance.

> This would be issued on an annual basis and would require a determination as to whether the insurance had been purchased and was adequate, and only after that determination was made could the certification be completed. This would require the annual certification.[38]

The International Apple Association raised the issue of fees for service. While the current Secretary may not anticipate a significant fee, a future Secretary "might wish to put the contractors out of business" and could set an unreasonable sum.[39]

Senator Williams tended to agree. "My feeling is if there were a fee," he said, "it should be limited to taking care of the administrative costs...."[40]

Rulemaking Authority of the Secretary

"Eliminate the rulemaking authority...." stated a Farm Bureau spokesman. "The statute is complete in itself and requires no supplemental rulemaking authority."[41]

The rulemaking authority may have posed something of a dilemma for critics. On the one hand, many of the concepts "used in the bill are not clearly defined and will be given meaning only by regulation by the Secretary...." Conversely, the terms of the bill "... would permit the Secretary to require almost any kind of information he might desire" and "... could lead to the control of a large segment of domestic migrant farmworkers." This "broad ... grant of authority ... should be deleted."[42]

"We feel," asserted Robert Rea of the Virginia State Horticultural Society, "that it should be mandatory" for the Secretary to issue a certificate of registration as a migrant labor contractor to any person who files the required information and carries a reasonable amount of insurance. "The mere threat of withholding a certificate," Rea stated, "... places the labor contractor under direct control of the Secretary of Labor. This allows the Secretary to, in effect, dictate wage rates, housing and working conditions that the crew leader must agree to or be threatened with loss of the right to earn a livelihood." The proposal, "as written," he said, could "make the cure worse than the disease."[43]

Crossing State Boundaries

Concerning interstate commerce, Delmer Robinson's ranch straddled the Virginia-West Virginia frontiers. "You can almost figure that an employee of mine operating a wagon with 10 people on it going from one side of the orchard to the other is a migrant labor contractor, according to this definition. I am sure," he stated, "that is not what is meant" in the context of the legislation.[44]

The definition of contractor is so broad, stated Joseph Dorsey, Frederick County, Virginia, that it would "include any growers who hire and transport workers across State lines, which many of our members have to do daily in making use of labor within their various locations. Our association," by virtue of its location, "draws on several States for both regular and seasonal labor."[45] These definitions, stated another grower, are so broad that even a Greyhound bus would require registration if "10 or more" migrants were aboard.[46]

Financial Responsibility

During hearings in the House, Richard O'Connell, the National Council of Farmer Cooperatives, was asked,

> Is it not a fair and reasonable requirement to expect these crew leaders who transport families of workers from one State to another to be financially responsible to the migrant workers which they transport for personal injuries... and property damage?

O'Connell thought the requirement was appropriate if the question were, in fact, that explicit. However, O'Connell found the term "Financial Responsibility" to be obtuse and questioned whether it meant bonding. "This is one of these vague terms that if you start writing regulations on it it can mean anything."[47]

BRACEROS VERSUS DOMESTIC WORKERS

During the hearings of 1961, C. H. Fields (of the Farm Bureau of New Jersey) was questioned by Representative Herbert Zelenko (D-NY).

> Mr. FIELDS. ... New Jersey farmers do not use migrant labor because they want to. They would much prefer not to use it if there were any other labor available at a wage they could afford to pay....

> Mr. ZELENKO. You said the New Jersey farmer would not engage migrant labor if he could help it, but that he could not get local labor at the price he wants to pay.

> Mr. FIELDS. At the price that he can afford to pay, I said.

> Mr. ZELENKO. Would you be good enough to give this Committee ... what the prevailing wage is in New Jersey for a farm laborer doing the type of work that a migrant would do ...?

> Mr. FIELDS.... $1.10 an hour.[48]

> In the early 1960s, Congress had under consideration not only legislation dealing with farm labor contractors but, as well, with the braceros.[49] As it has evolved, the bracero program (and later, the H-2A program) has been based upon two premises.

(A) there are not sufficient workers who are able, willing, and qualified, and who will be available at the time and place needed, to perform the labor or services involved ...

(B) the employment of the alien in such labor or services will not adversely affect the wages and working conditions of workers in the United States similarly employed.[50]

An adverse effect wage rate was devised that must be paid to both foreign and domestic workers (where an effort has been made to employ the former), and which was intended, nominally, to prevent a negative impact from employment of braceros.

Comparing Braceros with Domestic Workers

Gradually, domestic employment and utilization of braceros became intertwined. "The documentation is clear," stated Vera Mayer, National Consumers' League, "that the massive importation of cheap foreign labor has lowered wages to American farmworkers and taken away job opportunities from them."[51] Labor Secretary Arthur Goldberg seemed to agree. "There is increasing evidence of the correlation between this large-scale use of foreign workers in agriculture and the employment situation of our own farmworkers." He stressed that the central problems of migrant farmworkers were the "lack of reasonably attractive employment opportunities" and "low wages."[52]

Here, the Secretary and Ms. Mayer were not alone. The Rev. John Wagner, associated with the National Council for the Spanish Speaking (of San Antonio), suggested that the impact of the bracero program "is very great." Father Wagner opined, "... it throws another large number of unskilled workers into a pool that is already overloaded with unskilled workers, and there becomes a mad scramble for jobs."[53] Meanwhile, Father James Vizzard, then associated with the National Catholic Rural Life Conference, posed the question: "What other group of farmers or workers have to compete in the marketplace with ... workers brought into this country by an agency of the Government, partly at taxpayers' expense?"[54]

Triggs of the Farm Bureau explained that the "... domestic worker is often severely disabled, physically, mentally, or psychiatrically or by reason of age. In such cases," he stated, "the employer should not be required to pay the same wages as for an able bodied man. Whereas," he added, "the Mexican workers are carefully screened, they are mostly young, vigorous, able bodied."[55] Twiggs added, "If the farmer prepays transportation for Mexican nationals it is with the assurance that the worker will not leave the job after he arrives to work for somebody else." Further, he stated, the Mexican workers "are unaccompanied by their families" and, as a result, "they need barracks type housing." Finally, he stated, "... the hours of employment are generally uniform and standardized."[56]

Both labor and management witnesses seemed in agreement with respect to domestic and Mexican crews. Arnold Mayer, of the Amalgamated Meat Cutters and Butcher Workmen of North America (AFL-CIO), stated:

In the first place, the bracero is very docile, more so than even the domestic migrants are. Over the bracero's head hangs the threat that he may be sent back to Mexico if he complains too much or if he kicks up too much of a fuss. He has left his family, he expects to come back with some money, so he does not want to be sent back without money.

Mayer agreed that the "bracero is carefully screened so that the workers that do come from Mexico are prime labor." As "single men," the braceros have an impact on housing. "The growers can erect barrack-type housing for them." American migrants "very often move with their families and housing and facilities for them are more expensive." Mayer stated, "... the growers know that this importation causes a surplus of labor and that this surplus is very, very useful in keeping wage rates down." And, rather than "compete for labor," the foreign workers are simply made available.[57]

Sorting Out the Workers

"There is a clear interrelationship between the administration of the migratory labor program and the administration of Public Law 78 [the bracero program]," stated Secretary Wirtz. If we can put domestic labor on a sounder administrative basis, "which this bill would help us very much to do, it would mean a lesser need for the use of Mexican nationals...." He referred to the "floating group of American migratory workers" and observed, "I feel quite strongly that the proper use of the crew leader can be of real advantage to the employing farmer as well as to the employees."[58]

During hearings in 1963, Representative Thomas Gill (D-HI) entered into a dialogue with Richard Shipman of the National Farmers Union. Gill observed that undocumented farm workers were sometimes cheated out of their earnings. Shipman replied, "Of course, if a person is in this country illegally, he is at the mercy of anybody, they have no rights...." Gill concurred: "... they are fair game for a shoddy operator."[59] In some parts of Oregon, Gill speculated, undocumented labor makes up about 20% of the workforce. In that particular region of Oregon, Representative Roosevelt stated, "practically all of the recruiting was done for a sugar company."[60]

Shipman concurred that the "wetback problem is of long standing." He stated: "In the total Spanish-speaking migrant group, approximately 20 percent enter the United States on 'border crosser permits' ... on forged documents, or in the old-fashioned wetback manner." Licensing would help. Roosevelt suggested that, under the current proposal, suspension would follow if the contractor "has recruited, employed or utilized the service of a person with knowledge that such a person is violating the provisions of the immigration and nationality laws." Such a person can be refused a license, but is also "subject to penalty under the Act." He further pointed to a provision allowing the Secretary, under authority to obtain information, to conduct a more specific investigation.[61]

CONGRESSIONAL ACTION ON CONTRACTOR REGISTRATION

During the late 1950s and early 1960s, Senator Williams had sought controls on farm labor contractors, and, though the measures were not adopted, he kept trying. In 1963, legislation began to move. The contractor registration bill was called up for Senate consideration on June 11, 1963. Williams explained the nature of farm labor contracting, concluding that many contractors "perform their functions in [a] satisfactory and responsible manner" — but that others "have exploited both farmers and workers."[62]

At that point, Senator John Tower (R-TX) objected to passage of the bill, stating, "I do not believe the measure is needed." Tower agreed that there were "occasional instances of crew leaders who don't deal fairly with workers or farmers," but these cases "are disputable" and "exaggerated." Since many states already register farm labor contractors, the proposed legislation would be redundant, he stated.[63] No other Senator rose in opposition, and the Senate moved on to other business. A few minutes later, the Senate switched back to the farm labor contractor legislation and, following a brief discussion, passed the bill on a voice vote.[64]

It was more than a year before Representative Roosevelt called up the measure in the House. The bill, he declared, was "essentially noncontroversial."[65] Representative Gill, the author of the bill, agreed that the bill was "a very minimal piece of legislation" but "the need for this ... is very obvious." Gill stated,

These crew chiefs deal with a type of labor ... which is often undereducated or in many instances completely uneducated. The literacy level is generally low. Their ability to understand their rights is ... minimal.

Many of these migrant laborers have no voting residence. They have no Congressman ... nor do they have access to other officials who may help them with their problems. Therefore, they are easy to victimize.

The bill "... would be of great assistance to the good crew leaders ... the vast majority. It will prevent them from being daubed with the same brush used on the bad."[66]

Indeed, the bill was noncontroversial. Representative Robert Griffin (R-MI) rose "in support of this legislation." Representative Charles Bennett (D-FL) similarly expressed his "strong support" of the bill. "The migrant laborer should no longer be neglected," stated Representative William Fitts Ryan (D-NY). "This bill is belated recognition of his plight."[67]

Thereupon, the House passed the farm labor contractor registration legislation by 343 yeas to 7 nays, though with several changes from the Senate-passed version.[68] As amended, the bill was taken up in the Senate, passed by voice vote, and sent to President Lyndon Johnson, becoming P.L. 88-582 on September 7, 1964.[69]

THE FARM LABOR CONTRACTOR REGISTRATION ACT OF 1964

Congress finds, the act began, that "certain irresponsible contractors," by their activities in the migrant labor field, have "impeded, obstructed, and restrained" the flow of interstate commerce. Thus, Congress mandates that "all persons engaged in the activity of contracting for the services of workers for interstate agricultural employment comply with the provisions of this act and all regulations prescribed hereunder by the Secretary of Labor."[70] In general, the act provided the following:

Definitions

- "The term 'farm labor contractor' means any person, who, for a fee, either for himself or on behalf of another person, recruits, solicits, hires, furnishes, or transports ten or more migrant workers ... at any one time in any calendar year for interstate agricultural employment."

- "Such term shall not include (1) any nonprofit charitable organization, public or nonprofit private education institution, or similar organization; (2) any farmer, processor, canner, ginner, packing shed operator, or nurseryman who engages in any such activity for the purpose of supplying migrant workers solely for his own operation; (3) any full-time or regular employee of any entity referred to in (1) or (2) above; or (4) any person who engages in any such activity for the purpose of obtaining migrant workers of any foreign nation for employment in the United States, if the employment of such workers is subject to (A) an agreement between the United States and such foreign nation, or (B) an arrangement with the government of any foreign nation under which written contracts for the employment of such workers are provided for and the enforcement thereof is provided for in the United States by an instrumentality of such foreign nation."

- " 'State' means any of the States of the United States, the District of Columbia, the Virgin Islands, the Commonwealth of Puerto Rico, and Guam."

- " 'Migrant worker' is a term that means an individual whose primary employment is in agriculture ... or who performs agricultural labor ... on a seasonal or other temporary basis."

Certificate of Registration Requirement

- "No person shall engage in activities as a farm labor contractor unless he first obtains a certificate of registration from the Secretary, and unless such certificate is in full force and effect and is in such person's immediate possession."

- The act observes of a "full-time or regular employee" holding a valid certificate of registration: "Any such employee shall be required to have in his immediate personal possession when engaging in such activities such identification as the Secretary may require showing such employee to be an employee of, and duly authorized to engage in activities as a farm labor contractor for, a person holding a valid certificate of registration under the provisions of this Act."

- "Any such [regular or full-time] employee shall be subject to the provisions of this Act and regulations prescribed hereunder to the same extent as if he were required to obtain a certificate or registration in his own name."

Issuance of Certificate of Registration

- The Secretary shall issue a certificate of registration to any person who "has executed and filed with the Secretary" whatever documents "the Secretary may require in order effectively to carry out the provisions of this Act;" has filed with the Secretary documentation "satisfactory to the Secretary of the financial responsibility of the applicant" with respect to motor vehicles; and "has filed ... a set of his fingerprints."
- "The Secretary may refuse to issue, and may suspend, revoke, or refuse to renew a certificate of registration to any farm labor contractor if he finds that such contractor" (inter alia):

  — knowingly has given false or misleading information to migrant workers concerning the terms, conditions, or existence of agriculture employment
  — has failed, without justification, to perform agreements entered into or arrangements with farm operators
  — has failed, without justification, to comply with the terms of any working arrangement he has made with migrant workers
  — has failed to show financial responsibility satisfactory to the Secretary ... or has failed to keep in effect a policy of insurance required by subsection (a)(2) of this section
  — has recruited, employed, or utilized the services of a person with knowledge that such person is violating the provisions of the immigration and nationality laws of the United States
  — has been convicted of any crime under State or Federal law
  — has failed to comply with any of the provisions of this Act or any regulations issued hereunder."

- "A certification of registration ... shall be effective for the remainder of the calendar year during which it is issued, unless suspended or revoked by the Secretary as provided in this Act. A certificate of registration may be renewed each calendar year upon approval by the Secretary of an application for its renewal."

Obligations and Prohibitions

- The contractor will "ascertain and disclose to each worker at the time the worker is recruited the following information to the best of his knowledge and belief: (1) the area of employment, (2) the crops and operations on which he may be employed, (3) the transportation, housing, and insurance to be provided him, (4) the wage rates to be paid him, and (5) the charges to be made by the contractor for his services...."
- "Upon arrival at a given place of employment, post in a conspicuous place a written statement of the terms and conditions of that employment...."
- "In the event he manages, supervises, or otherwise controls the housing facilities, post in a conspicuous place the terms and conditions of occupancy...."
- In the event he pays migrant workers, to keep close and careful records of all transactions and to make them generally available.

Authority To Obtain Information

- "The Secretary or his designated representative may investigate and gather data with respect to matters which may aid in carrying out the provisions of this Act." He "... may investigate and gather data respecting such case, and may, in connection therewith, enter and inspect such places and such records (and make such transcriptions thereof), question such persons, and investigate such facts, conditions, practices, or matters as may be necessary or appropriate to determine whether a violation of this Act has been committed."

Agreements with Federal and State Agencies

- The secretary is allowed to enter into compacts with various state and federal agencies with respect to enforcement of the act and related activities.

Penalty Provisions

- A penalty of not more than $500 is prescribed for violations of the act.

Judicial Review

- A limited system of judicial review is prescribed under the act.

Rules and Regulations

- "The Secretary is authorized to issue such rules and regulations as he determines necessary for the purposes of carrying out" certain provisions of this act.

Chapter 3

THE FIRST YEARS OF THE FARM LABOR CONTRACTOR REGISTRATION ACT (1964-1974)

From 1964 until 1974, the FLCRA was given institutional life. Administration of the act was set in motion and patterns of interpretation were developed. There was, however, some criticism of the act and a sense that it had not lived up to the hope and expectations of its authors.

THE INAUGURAL PERIOD

FLCRA focused upon one aspect of the issue of migrant and seasonal worker protections: the farm labor contractor. In late December 1964, Secretary Wirtz issued regulations under the act, and the Manpower Administrator, Bureau of Employment Security, was given the responsibility as the authorized designee of the Secretary.[71]

There followed a series of directives published in the *Federal Register* dealing with insurance and financial responsibility.[72] However, some terms used in the legislation seem to have lent themselves to vague patterns of interpretation. For example, see the definition of farm labor contractor.

The term 'farm labor contractor' means any person ... [who] recruits, solicits, hires, furnishes, or transports ten or more migrant workers ... at any one time in any calendar year for interstate agricultural employment.

The official interpretation of the statute explores each of these concepts at some length but, seemingly, without resolution.[73]

In 1969, under Secretary George Shultz, DOL underwent administrative restructuring with FLCRA (and 28 other programs) assigned to the Assistant Secretary for Manpower.[74] Then, in 1972, under Secretary James Hodgson, a split was effected with the labor standards aspects of FLCRA assigned to the Wage/Hour Division in the Employment Standards Administration. For more general administration, authority was left with the Assistant Secretary for Manpower.[75] Under the act, the Secretary was permitted to enter into a cooperative agreement with state authorities where the states had roughly comparable laws. Where there might be a refusal to authorize (or re-authorize) issuance of a certificate of registration, a hearing would be scheduled before the Solicitor (after 1973, the Associate Solicitor) of DOL or his designee.[76] For a marginally educated farm labor contractor (if that assessment were true), one might expect the total impact to have been a little confusing.[77]

A Certain Dissatisfaction

FLCRA had not been entirely successful. "Complaints have grown through the years," observed Senator Gaylord Nelson (D-WI), "that this first effort of the Congress was lacking in several areas...."[78]

During 1973 and 1974, further hearings were conducted on the issue. The current system, some suggested, "... has been the source of massive abuse and exploitation of agricultural workers." Though Congress had recognized the problem with adoption of FLCRA, the abuses have shown "no signs of moderating."[79] No matter "how strong the vote in the Congress, it [farmworker legislation] usually seems to be filed away in some cubbyhole without any appropriations, without any committee staff, and the result in almost all cases has been nonenforcement." In the "9 years of the existence of this bill," it was suggested, there "has been no enforcement. It has been totally ineffective. It has been a dud."[80]

Problems Associated with FLCRA

New legislation may take time to work through various impediments: FLCRA was no exception. From the testimony before the House and Senate Committees, it was clear that problems were numerous.

A Lack of Penalties

The Departments of Labor and Justice seemed to feel "that present penalties are insufficient to deter repeated violations," and this "deters them from pressing prosecutions," a witness stated, urging "greater penalties."[81]

Representative Augustus Hawkins (D-CA) posed the question to a group of DOL Administrators: Bernard DeLury, Assistant Secretary for Employment Standards; Warren Landis, Acting Administrator, Wage/Hour Division; and Eugene Bonfiglio, Chief, Branch of Farm Labor Contractor Registration.

> Mr. HAWKINS. What is the penalty at the present time for failure to register?
>
> Mr. LANDIS. There is no specific penalty in the present law, unless there is a willful violation, and then the present law provides a fine of up to $500.
>
> Mr. HAWKINS. Has anyone been fined, and if so, how many?
>
> Mr. LANDIS. I think one....
>
> Mr. BONFIGLIO. Since the act became operative in January 1965, we have had four cases that went to criminal court for prosecution. Of those four, two were thrown out by the Justice Department, and two were finally prosecuted and fined $100 in each case, and in one of the cases the fine was lifted.
>
> Mr. HAWKINS.... I assume that under the law those who commit violations can either have their registration revoked or other penalties imposed. Can you give us any idea how many registrations have been revoked.
>
> Mr. DeLURY. None, sir. Mr. HAWKINS. None. Mr. DeLURY. None this year. What about last year?
>
> Mr. BONFIGLIO. Last year we revoked three certificates and suspended two, I believe. We had one employee who was denied based on a past criminal action.

A DOL spokesman stepped in to explain. The record "does not mean that crew leaders are not violating [the law] or that we are not attempting to enforce the law. Under the regulations ... the due process is required, we have to notify the crew leader that we intend to revoke this certificate and give him time to request a hearing." Then, there is the time factor. "If he requests a hearing ... the time element usually goes beyond his stay in one place, and by that time he is gone or the end of the season is on us." Landis then observed that unless the violation "is pretty bad we think it is better to get him into compliance and let him continue his work...." The dialogue moved on.

> Mr. HAWKINS. Well, the problem itself is not evaporating though; is it?

> Mr. LANDIS. No sir. There still is a problem for the migrant workers, a big problem.[82]

Lack Of Staff

In response to Representative Hawkins, it was noted that there were probably about 5,000 interstate crew leaders and another 3,000 intrastate crew leaders. The figures "are not accurate," Landis observed. "They are the best estimates that we could make." And, Landis continued, "... a little under 2,000" are registered.[83]

With more than eight years of experience under the act, Mr. Hawkins queried, "Are you making any effort to see that those who are not registered become registered? Who does the job of enforcing that?" Landis replied, "Well, that is our job, of course, to register them and to call them to account when they are not registered." DOL was trying to deal with that "through investigations" and "through public service announcements on radio and TV ... in both English and Spanish."[84]

We are not here "to be critical of you gentlemen," Representative William Ford (D-MI) stated, when introducing the Department witnesses, but "to determine whether ... we can find a way to make the law finally do what it was originally intended to do."[85] However, a certain amount of criticism did emerge.

The 1963 Act "was never enforced because the bureaucrats who were given the responsibility to enforce it did not get out of the regional offices," argued Elijah Boone of the Community Action Migrant Program in Immokalee, Florida. He alleged that most of DOL's staff (where crew leaders were concerned) were recycled "from old rural manpower, which had already been shown to be ineffective."[86] Alcario Samudia, now with the Wisconsin Department of Labor, recalled that when the crew leader Act came into being in 1963, "... I registered ... but then we found out that the Government did not have anybody to enforce the new laws, so many of us did not even bother to register" after that.[87] "It is a law," explained Barbara Rhine, an attorney for the United Farm Workers, "that everyone here claims and knows is not enforced."[88]

Was the act fatally flawed? Or were enforcement officials jaded? Might the problem have more to do with appropriations? According to Luke Danielson, a former investigator for the Colorado Migrant Legal Services Agency, DOL officials had advised him that "they lack[ed] sufficient investigative staff to process complaints" — which resulted in this "abominable enforcement record."[89] Again:

> Mr. FORD. How many field enforcement people were actually involved in trying to check registrations ... of crew leaders prior to October 1972?
>
> Mr. BONFIGLIO. We had five field men in 1972. In 1965, we had 40. In 1966, that dropped to 17, and each year after that it declined down to 1972 when we had 5.[90]

Elsewhere, Representative Ford concluded, "It would appear that if we were operating with five people throughout the country to enforce this, knowing that we have in excess of 6,000 possible people to be policed, that we have not very aggressively ..." gone about enforcement of the statute.[91]

Other Issues

Clearly, other problems dogged enforcement of FLCRA during its first 10 years rendering the act either unenforceable or, perhaps, innocuous. Among allegations were the following:

The Language Question. Investigators were not always fluent in the language spoken by the workers: Spanish, particularly in the West. Though some announcements appear to have been made in Spanish, the cultural division was such that, often, they were inappropriately positioned. Even in terms of payment and Social Security, the pay stub may have been written in English, which "people don't understand."[92]

Crew Leader Versus Grower. There had been, through the decade, an intermittent conflict between the grower and the crew leader. If we could just "make the grower responsible," Landis stated for DOL, "... this would be the biggest boost to getting these crew leaders registered."[93] Conversely, Daniel Boone of the United Farm Workers charged that labor contractors "are used by the real employers, the growers, to maximize the insecurity of the worker" by adding yet another level of authority. The grower (farmer or company) "by the use of the contractor has insulated itself from any responsibility" for payment, insurance, and related costs associated with migratory employment.[94] Luke Danielson argued "If the crew leader is not in fact registered, make the farmer liable for the wrongdoings of the crew leader."[95]

Inflating Crew Levels. Guadalupe Murguia, a United Farm Worker rank-and-filer, testified that contractors exploit the growers by padding their payrolls with grandchildren and great-grandchildren. "As an example, we discovered that the contractors had people on their lists who had been dead for 4 or 5 years." Where there is contract work, the company "pays for the people that the contractor has on his payroll."[96] Pablo Espinosa, also a rank-and-filer, affirmed, "I used to work for a labor contractor where he used to come and tell me, put two or three more people on the books. Put so and so and so on. Well, so and so don't exist, I would say. Well, you put them on. Who pays for that? The grower."[97]

Inspector/Grower Collusion? There was a sense, among some workers, that inspectors had become an adjunct to the growers. They, the inspectors, were educated and, often, spoke a language different from the field workers. When abuses were complained of, the inspectors "let them know that they are coming" to inspect, which, from the workers' perspective, tended to stack the deck against honest inspection. "It doesn't do any good to report anybody," observed Jessie de la Cruz of the United Farm Workers. "Nothing is done about it."[98] It was only by contacting inspectors "on repeated occasions," Danielson noted, "that we were able to get them to take this complaint at all."[99] Again, "There is no incentive to understand the Act as contractors know that the Act is not being enforced."[100]

AMENDING THE STATUTE

In some respects, FLCRA appeared to have had little impact. Demands for its repeal (during the early years) seem to have been few.

"... I think it is appropriate for me to express a kind of personal 'mea culpa,'" suggested Father James Vizzard, an early backer of FLCRA. In the early 1960s, he stated that "under the leadership of Senator Harrison Williams and his Senate Migratory Labor Subcommittee, we were able to formulate and pass this legislation...." But, he added: "Hindsight tells us now that, despite a great deal of good will and technical competence, we really didn't do a very good job of it." Father Vizzard opined,

> First, at the time there was no organized grassroots body with sufficient knowledge and experience to advise us of the day-to-day realities of farm worker problems in all parts of our country. Despite extensive studies and hearings it still was principally a group of us here in Washington ... who did what we thought best, and as it turned out that wasn't good enough.

Second, once a legislative battle had been won and a bill passed, our forces tended to disperse and forgot the second half of the battle, namely, appropriations. Almost every act we passed, therefore, was grossly underfunded and continues to be so even to this day.

Third, and perhaps most important of all, we failed to build into the program adequate and continuous enforcement. Without any exception that I can recall, the agencies charged with enforcement have never done a satisfactory or, in very many cases, even an honest job of enforcing these laws passed by Congress.[101]

Amendments would bring forth a new phase (and, in some respects, a more turbulent phase) of the regulation of agricultural labor. As revision of the statute proceeded, a number of issues emerged: some old, others new.

Changing Character of the Farm Labor Contractor

During hearings in the early 1960s, the farm labor contractor had been somewhat disparaged. A decade later, that view had mellowed. There were still tales of "short-counts" and beatings of workers who ran into "disfavor" with the crew chief — but these were issues with which DOL did not seem to become involved.[102]

"The great majority of these people," suggested C. H. Fields of the Farm Bureau, "are responsible businessmen who have made a significant investment in their businesses and who make every effort to abide by the law." Again:

... these people are small businessmen; they operate under extremely difficult circumstances; they do not have the services of accountants, bookkeepers, or legal advisors; and the more paperwork that is required the more apt they are to call it quits and go out of business.[103]

Definitional elements entered the picture as well. Elijah Boone of the Community Migrant Action Program (Immokalee, Florida) said that there were different kinds of crew leaders. "A contractor might be a very well to do, upper middle-class white businessman, who has money to invest in necessary machinery that a farm worker would know of." The contractor might be the person in charge of the contract and "... then he would hire the crew leader who would recruit the labor...."[104] Who might be charged with the payment of the workers (and with making deductions for Social Security and related matters) seems to have been unclear.

Defining a Labor Dispute or Strike

Immigration officials, argued Father Vizzard, appear "to be in the pocket of large-scale employers," while "notorious labor contractors have been allowed repeatedly to build up their strike-breaking crews with these known illegals recruited throughout the Southwest."[105] Dan Pollitt, now special counsel to the Subcommittee, questioned Vizzard. A contractor, Pollitt suggested, was required to explain to contract workers "where they are going, wages, housing conditions, and so on." Pollitt asked, "Do you think it would be helpful to add that you must also say whether or not there is a strike going on or whether a contract is at its last stages of negotiations." Father Vizzard responded: "Yes. I would."[106]

But again, there were problems. Guinn Sinclair, president, National Farm Labor Contractors Association, suggested an almost "complete lack of legislation" on labor-management relations in the agricultural field as to what "constitutes a labor dispute." Sinclair questioned: "Why should a contractor be the judge when our courts have issued conflicting decisions?" And: "Does a labor dispute exist when the United Farm Workers Union issues a boycott of lettuce and table grapes?" Or, again, when the Teamsters or the United Farm Workers, then in a contest for farmworker loyalties, "claim jurisdiction and yet no laws exist to determine the will of the workers themselves?" Sinclair protested, "... I don't think the contractor should be the one to decide that there is a dispute."[107]

The Farm Bureau argued that agriculture "is exempt from the National Labor Relations Act and farmers have no legal method to deal with labor disputes" and "unfair labor practices." Again, there were definitional issues: "... what constitutes a strike, slowdown or labor-management dispute," and when does "such a condition exist at a particular farm." Were a farmer to become engaged in such issues, the proposal "could have the effect of determining whether or not his crop would be harvested." The Bureau continued, "Fruits and vegetables tend to reach the harvest stage as determined by the inexorable laws of nature," and a farm "cannot wait around until someone," perhaps the state or the federal government, "decides whether there is a legally-constituted strike or labor dispute." The provision, it stated, "would seem to be an unworkable and unreasonable responsibility" to place upon contractors.[108]

DeLury of DOL took a cautious attitude, suggesting that the provision was "pretty broad" as written.[109] Later, Bruce Burkdoll, speaking for the Central California Farmers Association, charged that "a union or group of workers" could create "a labor dispute, even though the union does not represent" the workers involved. He concluded, "... just because a student or someone else that never saw you on your ranch stops in front and waves a flag, we just cannot live with that."[110]

The *Day Haul* and the *Shape-Up*

The *shape-up* exists in most regions from which growers or contractors recruit. "That is the place where the people gather to find out whether there will be work that day, sometimes as early as 2 a.m....." The shape-up varies from one locality to another. So does the nature of the work sought.[111]

"The contractor ... will have the pick of the lot," according to Barbara Rhine, United Farm Workers attorney. "He will choose the strong, the young, the healthy.... Or the attractive women who have to turn a pretty face and act at the driver's bidding ... Or the illegal alien, whom he can have taken back by the border patrol before he pays the day's wages." If the character of the work is marginal, "then the shape-up area will be filled with the local winos, the sad, stumbling men and women who are so abject that all it takes is the promise of wine to get them into the fields." Rhine stated,

> And so the people get on the buses and hard-seated trucks and try to sleep on their way to work. If they get miles into the fields and find that it's not the first picking that they have been promised, or that there are no toilets and drinking water, or that the gloves to protect their hands are torn, missing, or not provided at all, then their choice is to work anyhow or walk back to town and miss the whole day. If they complete the day's work, they frequently get paid less than the promise, and with deductions made for fees and transportation.

Further, she alleged that "If they get their slips showing the deductions for social security and disability, they find out later when they are old and sick that the money somehow never found its way to the proper State or Federal agency."[112]

Rhine's comments focused upon California, but, Theodore Dietz of the New Jersey Department of Community Affairs explained the conditions of *day-haul* workers in his part of the country — casual workers employed on a daily basis.

- Both federal and state minimum wage laws are consistently broken.

- "Many crew leaders go unregistered." They disguise their function as crew leaders by using a number of cars and "by carrying less than ten people per vehicle."
- The crew leader provides "either insufficient information or misinformation" to the worker. "Because there is no written contract between the crew leader and worker, the worker may agree to pick one crop and end up picking another at a different piece rate."
- "Social Security deductions are never made for day haul workers, eliminating many of them from eligibility when they reach 65."
- No statement of earnings, deductions or hours worked is provided to the worker.
- "Day haul workers rarely are provided toilet facilities in the field and occasionally no water...."
- Children of a very young age are a part of the system.
- "Arbitrary dismissals and blacklisting" are part of the day haul system.
- "No protective clothing against weeds, rain or pesticides are ever provided...." ! "No health or first aid services are available to day haul workers."[113]

Proposed amendments tended to exclude day haul workers. Father Vizzard (now of the United Farm Workers) expressed concern. "Our experience," he stated, "tells us that some of the grossest abuses against both farm workers and employers are perpetrated by day haulers." The rationale for this exemption is "'because there are so few inspectors.' We think that the proper response to this fact is ... a notable increase in enforcement staff."[114] David Sweeney, Political and Legislative Director for the Teamsters, agreed. "We concur with the statement made by the United Farm Workers in their testimony ... 'We think that the proper response to this fact is, as stated above, a notable increase in the enforcement staff.'"[115] Further, Dietz observed that exclusion of day hauling left him "in a word, dumbfounded."[116]

Even DeLury affirmed DOL's opposition to eliminating day haulers from coverage. "This exclusion would deprive laborers working for a day-haul contractor of guaranteed insurance protection and basic information about the job. These guarantees," DeLury stated, "are as important to the day worker as to the laborer who works for a contractor over an extended period."[117]

The Administration, however, was divided on the issue. Jack Donnachie, Rural Manpower Service, DOL, raised the issue of practicality. "We do have some points where we supervise day haul, as well as they can be supervised," Donnachie stated. But he cautioned that "... you are out on a public corner with a day haul" and you "cannot stop a man," he argued, when the recruitment takes place in a public space. "We received a lot of criticism ... for day haul operations and justifiably so," he stated, "... so we are getting out of the day haul business as fast as we can get out because we cannot control it."[118]

As the hearings progressed, Representative Ford noted a certain level of caution. If day haulers were included in the bill, "... it is obvious that we are going to be picking up ... a situation that for some period of time would require constant day-by-day monitoring." He continued:

> Mr. FORD. So we are talking about more manpower than we have heretofore been using. Do you have any idea about what your additional manpower needs would be, taking into account the additional enforcement power of the Act. Have you given that any thought.

> Mr. DeLURY. Yes, we have. Recently we went up before Mr. [Daniel] Flood's Appropriations Subcommittee and requested a supplemental budget for the Employment Standards Administration, and in the area of farm labor contractor registration work we ear-marked ... 10 additional positions for the coming years."[119]

In an aside to Father Vizzard, Ford stated that "... there was not any intent on the part of the authors of this bill to diminish our capacity to deal with the problem" of day haulers: "... we are just trying to deal in priorities with the resources we have."[120]

Interstate Versus Intrastate

The original labor contractor legislation focused upon interstate transportation of migrant and seasonal workers. Ben Robertson of the Wage/Hour Division explained that Florida crew leaders, under current law, "would not need to be registered ... until they indicated or got ready to move North. They would then come under the coverage of the act because of the interstate character of the work."[121]

An amendment to the act proposed to cover interstate intrastate operations. Fr. Vizzard applauded the new section, noting that "many — and I would say perhaps most — of the contractors operate wholly within one state. It is long overdue that they be covered by the provisions of the law."[122] DeLury was equally supportive.[123] And Alcario Samudia, the former crew leader from Wisconsin, urged that all crew leaders "who recruit interstate or intrastate[,] regardless of whether they only recruit for themselves or a combination of employers," be registered.[124]

Fields of the Farm Bureau argued against this expansion. "We strongly urge that it be made clear ... that it is not the intent of Congress to cover the intrastate activities of farm labor contractors," he stated.[125] George Sorn, of the Florida Fruit and Vegetable Association, urged that FLCRA continue to apply "only to crew leaders who cross state lines." Sorn stated that registration of other workers would be a "needless expenditure of taxpayers' money." He continued: "We believe leaders who operate only on an intrastate basis should not become subject to the Federal Act in those states which have adequate crew leader laws of their own."[126]

Establishing Responsibility: Growers Versus Farm Labor Contractors

In FLCRA, as originally adopted, a "farmer, processor, canner, ginner, packing shed operator, or nurseryman who engaged in" farm labor recruitment "solely for his own operations," shall not be included within the concept of a *farm labor contractor*.[127] Under the proposed amendments, the issue was raised anew.

There was a sense, among advocates of a stronger FLCRA, that growers had, by use of the contractor, "insulated" themselves from responsibility for a diverse range of employer-associated responsibilities.[128] At the same time, it was argued that the farm labor contractor does not set policy but, rather, merely follows orders laid down by growers. In south Texas, it was explained, the contractor does not set the rate of pay or determine the hours of work. He merely follows established policy and is nothing more, in effect, "than a crew foreman."[129] Barbara Rhine of the United Farm Workers explained that "whoever recruits labor for the grower is nothing more or less than his employee...."[130]

Some were willing to assign the contractor the role of an employee of the grower. DeLury of Labor, however, supported a provision in the draft bill making "growers liable for damages resulting from acts or omissions of unregistered farm labor contractors with whom they have contracted for services." He also recommended "a provision to prohibit outright the use of unregistered crew leaders by growers."[131] Joseph McAuliffe of the Wage/Hour Division noted an absence of responsibility. Someone, "we don't care which," has to assume responsibility.[132]

This issue, grower versus contractor, would remain central to the debate on FLCRA through the next decade. Much agricultural work seems to have been conducted on a quasi-cash basis. Or, where there were more formal processes, it may have been unrealistic to expect a worker, thirty years hence, to attempt to prove that he or she actually worked, for what period, and what was (or was not) taken out of his pay. Pay stubs may be written in English and may be basically unintelligible for non-English speaking workers. Given the migratory character of such workers, compensation information may well have been lost with the passage of time.[133]

Immigration and Adverse Effcet

Section 5(b)(6) of FLCRA provided that the Secretary might "refuse to issue" or "suspend, revoke, or refuse to renew a certificate of registration" if the farm labor contractor had "with knowledge" hired workers in violation of the immigration and nationality laws of the United States.

As the 1974 amendment moved through the legislative process, there was an effort to restructure this provision. Everyone, it seems, knew that undocumented aliens were employed in American agriculture but, beyond that awareness, there seemed little agreement as to a course to follow. Father Vizzard concluded: "It is too easy for the crew leader or labor contractor to escape the impact of that section of the law by simply claiming innocence, and who can prove to the contrary?"[134]

Much of the discussion focused upon knowledge. Rudy Juarez, a former farm worker experienced with crew leading operations, suggested that "contractors and the farmers [they represent] are heavily recruiting illegals from Mexico. Many times we have reported this to the border patrol," Juarez stated, "but they do not seem to be interested until the harvest is over." Senator Nelson inquired of Juarez: "I understand you to say that the employers frequently pay transportation of the illegals." Juarez replied, "Yes, sir. For many years I was a contractor myself."[135]

With one witness after another, though from different perspectives, the issue of use of undocumented workers was raised. Identity papers, it was alleged, were easy to acquire; but, once armed with fraudulent documents, who was to judge? "Since the Border Patrol cannot determine who is an illegal in the United States," opined Guinn Sinclair, "we do not feel you should impose upon the contractor the absolute law that he should know." Sinclair and Nelson discussed the problem of identification. "You know," Sinclair suggested to Nelson, "that the magnitude of Mexicans working in the United States is much greater than I think is conceived here." Part of the problem, the farm labor contractor suggested, rests with the governments of the United States and of Mexico. But, notwithstanding the source of the problem, "the contractor has no way of knowing who should be here and who should not be here."[136]

Mabel Mascarenas, wife of a farm labor contractor, questioned the "should know" proposal. "Are people going to wear a sign that says 'I am an alien,' or are we expected to act as Immigration Officers and know all the details of immigration papers?" Much of the work on the farms deals with perishable commodities. "When we need people, and people come to us seeking work,"she said, "we hire them. We are the most integrated business in America."[137]

"It is our view," suggested Joseph Phelan, National Council of Agricultural Employers, "that the imposition of the provision prohibiting the employment of illegal aliens would be tantamount to transferring to the employer a responsibility which correctly lies with the Immigration and Nationalization Service."[138] The Farm Bureau took a similar position. "On the surface," it noted, the premise, "'know or should know' to be in violation of the immigration laws," some may find appealing. But, "the question arises as to how a labor contractor is expected to know or determine whether a given worker is in this country illegally." The bill "is silent with regard to any procedure a contractor would be expected to follow." We urge "that this subsection be deleted." And it further stated: "The Immigration Service itself has not been too successful in stopping illegal entries or discovering those who enter illegally."[139]

Father Vizzard seemed unimpressed with arguments for use of illegals. He suggested that if one were "to raise the wages and improve the working conditions" under which aliens worked, American workers would be found. "When that happens traditionally in any part of American economic life, there are American workers to do the jobs." The system, he stated, "... is simply a fraud and the disguise has to be stripped back again and again and again."[140]

A NEW STATUTE THROUGH AMENDMENT

Although the issues raised during hearings on revision of FLCRA were of substance, they seem to have attracted relatively little attention. With hearings concluded, the Congress moved on to enactment of the farm labor amendments of 1974.

Bipartisanship Emerges in the House

In March 1974, Representative Ford introduced a nonpartisan bill incorporating the findings of the hearings — at least as they were understood.[141] Ford thanked Earl Landgrebe (R-IN), especially, for helping to invoke "a spirit of bipartisanship" that has resulted in a "unanimous vote" in committee. The bill is "cosponsored by every member of the Subcommittee on Agricultural Labor" and by other members on each side of the aisle.[142]

Bipartisan support was evident. "H.R. 13342 provides," explained James O'Hara (D-MI), "for stiffer penalties ... A civil remedy is made available in Federal court for those aggrieved under the act."[143] Frank Thompson (D-NJ), with others, emphasized that day haul workers would now be under the act.[144] The bill "broadens the definition of those covered," stated William Lehman (D-FL), "to include crew leaders recruiting for work done in the same State...."[145] Landgrebe affirmed that the Secretary will now "have an affirmative duty to monitor and investigate violations of the law." Both he and Albert Quie (R-MN) stressed that the grower will need to "observe a certificate of registration in the possession." At present, Representative Quie stated, "the crew leader is required to display it, but no one is required to observe it." Quie reassured the growers: "We are not attempting to make the growers joint employers with the crew leaders, nor are we attempting to make them responsible for the crew leader's unlawful actions."[146]

At the end of the colloquy, the rules were suspended and the bill was passed on a voice vote.[147] The following day, the bill was dispatched to the Senate where it was assigned to the Committee on Labor and Public Welfare.[148]

The Senate Concurs

It was October, six months later, before the bill reached the Senate floor. Then, the Senate moved to strike everything after the enacting clause and to insert its own language. Only two speakers addressed the issue, each expressing disenchantment with the original FLCRA. Recent testimony, observed Senator Williams, "... indicates that the act of 1963 has failed to achieve some of its original objectives."[149] Similarly, Senator Javits noted: "After 10 years of experience, ... we find that this act has largely been ignored and cannot be effectively enforced."[150]

While the provisions of the bill were briefly discussed, Senator Williams took note of "one new provision which I deem to be of such importance, that I wish to discuss it in some detail." Williams explained that farm labor contractors

> ... will be subject to a criminal penalty of up to a $10,000 fine or a prison sentence of up to 3 years (or both), if such contractor has knowingly engaged the services of an illegal alien. Illegal alien has been defined to mean any person who is an alien not lawfully admitted for permanent residence, or who has not been authorized by the Attorney General to accept employment....

> Illegal aliens have become an increasingly large source of farm labor in this country, and the services of a contractor are often utilized to procure this clandestine workforce. The existing act generally prohibits such activities by making it grounds for revoking or suspending the contractor's registration. However, if this tide of illegal immigration is to be stemmed, stricter enforcement and stronger penalties must be applied against those who violate the act. *These additional steps are necessary in light of the adverse effect such importation of illegal aliens has had on the wages and job security of our citizens, especially in times such as these of high unemployment.* (Italics added.)

Williams quoted Leonard Chapman of the Immigration and Naturalization Service. "'There are probably from six to 10 million illegal aliens in the country today. They are occupying jobs that unemployed Americans ought to have.'" No doubt, Williams asserted, "illegal farm labor would account for a sizable share."[151]

No one else spoke. Apparently regarded as routine, the bill was read a third time and passed on a voice vote, but in a form different from that of the House.[152]

Compromise Is Reached

The Senate-passed bill was sent back to the House where Representative Ford reported it. "Certain provisions in the Senate amendment," explained Mr. Landgrebe, "were very broad, would probably discourage registration, and possibly make the act more difficult to enforce." Landgrebe stated, "Since this is a 'crew leader' bill, *and not a bill covering farmers or growers*," certain adjustments seemed in order. (Italics added.) Representative Quie defended the growers. "The Senate version implicitly imposed upon growers and processors — all those with whom a labor contractor provided migrant workers — the obligation to enforce the act. In other words," Quie stated, "the Senate version held them responsible for the crew leaders' abuses and failures. We did not believe that it was necessary to hold a farmer criminally liable for the acts and omissions of another." He concluded, "... the responsibility for enforcing the act is where it belongs — on the Secretary of Labor and not on the farmer."[153] The new version retained the provisions concerning undocumented aliens.

Once again, the House voted to approve the measure on a voice vote and sent the new bill back to the Senate.[154] To this point, the two bodies had worked separately. No conference had been requested: none was deemed necessary. However, there now developed within the Senate a colloquy among Senators from the Pacific Northwest and from Florida.

Senator Mark Hatfield (R-OR) commenced. Out in the Pacific Northwest, "... we have a number of row crops and berries which lean heavily upon the use of student labor.... This is usually under the leadership of school teachers or other public education employees who take the responsibility of acting as crew leaders for these students" or are under the supervision of parents who, collectively, act "as crew leaders." Hatfield asked a question: Does the bill "include or does it exempt such cases as I have indicated — namely, teachers and public education employees and parents who act as crew leaders?" Second, does the bill as, currently drawn, include (or exclude) the permanent employee of the farmer (or, perhaps, the farmer himself) who hired these people? Senator Nelson, for the subcommittee, concurred with Senator Hatfield — and with Senator Warren Magnuson (D-WA) — in affirming that the Department of Labor was "not to consider this type of activity" when enforcing the act.[155]

A second colloquy occurred with Senator Lawton Chiles (D-FL). In the bill, the contractor could be exempt if his "recruitment activity is solely for his employer on no more than an incidental basis." Chiles agreed that "registration should be required of the individual whose sole job is to hire and recruit migrant labor" but he had concerns about the term "incidental." He stated: "I do not feel that the committee intended that regular employees who may perform some duties for their employer relative to securing migrant labor are to be required to register. It is my understanding," he stated, "that the bill aims at those who on a full-time basis hire or recruit migrant labor." Senator Nelson noted that "the purpose of this provision is to prevent farm labor contractors from avoiding registration by becoming the employee of each and every grower for whom they recruit and hire migrant workers...." But, *it was not the intent* of the act to include the "regular employee" of the grower. Chiles was not yet entirely clear. "Even though this duty might be considered to be an important aspect of his job responsibility by his employer ... , if he were a permanent employee and continued to have other duties, he would not be considered to have to register," Chiles inquired. "The Senator is absolutely correct in the manner in which he has stated it," Nelson replied.[156]

Following a summary statement by Senator Williams, the Senate concurred in the House-passed version of the bill. The vote was a voice vote.[157]

On October 19, President Gerald Ford returned the bill with a veto message. "This bill contains provisions designed to strengthen the protections of migrant farm workers ... which I support." But he noted that the Senate has added certain extraneous materials to the bill dealing with the federal personnel system. He directed that Congress remove them and promised to "approve" the bill as amended.[158] Senator Nelson had introduced S. 3202 in March 1974.[159] That bill was now resurrected, modified, and reported to the Senate on November 21[160] — and was adopted by a voice vote on November 22.[161] The House concurred (by a voice vote) on November 26.[162] On December 7, 1974, the bill was signed into law (P.L. 93-518).[163]

The 1974 FLCRA Amendments

The 1974 amendments represented a tightening up of the initial Farm Labor Contractor Registration Act. The focus was still primarily on the contractor. *Inter alia*, it provided the following:

- The concept of "interstate" was stricken, affirming by implication that the new act would apply as well to those persons operating within a state —but having an impact upon interstate commerce.
- The phrases "ten or more" and "at any one time in any calendar year" were deleted.
- It exempted from coverage any farmer or processor "who personally engages in any such activity."
- Similarly exempt was any full-time or regular employee "who engages in such activity solely for his employer *on no more than an incidental basis....*" (Italics added.)
- In order to deal with students and their elders (but to include day haul operators), there was added: "any person who engaged in any such activity (A) solely within a twenty-five-mile intrastate radius of his permanent place of residence and (B) for not more than thirteen weeks per year...."
- Added to the concept of agricultural employment was "the handling, planting, drying, packing, packaging, processing, freezing, or grading prior to delivery for storage of any agricultural or horticultural commodity in its unmanufactured state."
- "No person shall engage the services of any farm labor contractor ... unless he first determines that the farm labor contractor possesses a certificate from the Secretary that is in full force and effect at the time he contracts with the farm labor contractor."
- The applicant (contractor) must file a statement affirming that "each vehicle" and the "housing" to be used by migrants "conform to all applicable Federal and State safety and health standards" — to the extent that they are under "the applicant's ownership or control...."
- The applicant (contractor) shall designate the Secretary as his agent to accept "service summons" where he has departed from his original address/ jurisdiction or "has become unavailable to accept service...."
- The contractor must make known to the farm workers "the existence of a strike or other concerted stoppage, slowdown, or interruption of operations by employees at a place of contracted employment...."

- The contractor must "refrain from recruiting, employing, or utilizing, with knowledge, the services of any person, who is an alien not lawfully admitted for permanent residence or who has not been authorized by the Attorney General to accept employment...."

- Any agreement by an employee "to waive or to modify his rights" under the statute "shall be void as contrary to public policy" — except that a waiver to the Secretary for enforcement purposes is valid.

The rights and obligations of the several parties were spelled out in some detail.[164] Though certain segments of agriculture had reservations, the new amendments did not seem to represent a threat — and, indeed, they had been approved, repeatedly, with little debate and by voice vote.

Chapter 4

IMPLEMENTING A REVISED STATUTE (1974-1983)

By nearly all assessments, FLCRA had not been entirely successful in alleviating problems associated with migratory labor.[165] Revisions crafted during the 1973-1974 hearings brought some refinement of the statute. Few voices in Congress had been raised against the statute. Still, the act was not perceived as threatening to users of migrant workers.

PRESSURES BEGIN TO MOUNT

In October 1975, the House Subcommittee on Agricultural Labor conducted hearings on FLCRA. "As you may know," commenced Representative John McFall (D-CA), "my District in California includes the central part of the San Joaquin Valley. This is one of the most productive agricultural areas in the country, and as a result, agricultural labor is a vital part of the economic foundation of the area."[166]

McFall explained that DOL had failed "to adhere to ... clearly expressed Congressional intent" but had also failed "to provide its field personnel clear directions on the implementation of these [1974] amendments." It (DOL) had required "a farm or ranch foreman" to register as a farm labor contractor though he performed "many other duties" beyond worker recruitment. McFall had written to Labor Secretary John Dunlop but had not yet received a response. While he was "not opposed" to FLCRA or to the 1974 amendments ("I believe there is a need to ensure that farm labor is not exploited by labor contractors," he said.), his concern was over the DOL's failure "to provide an equitable and clearly defined implementation of the Act."[167]

Prior to the 1974 amendments, the focus had been on the plight of agricultural workers. Now, it shifted to employers and to the structure of the industry. The wrong people, it was argued, were being caught up in the Department's net.

GENERAL PROBLEMS OF ADMINISTRATION

We have had "statements of concern" (and "some compliments") that DOL was "too vigorous in its administration of the act" — and, conversely, that it "is not vigorous enough," stated Chairman Ford of the House Agricultural Labor Subcommittee. The Congress has "used every device possible," he noted, "... to prod, criticize, and sometimes castigate the Labor Department to push for vigorous enforcement of laws." Still, the Committee does not want to "make compliance with the law so unpalatable" that we end up "litigating while farmworkers receive no real factual benefits from the enactment of the legislation."[168] Regulations had not yet been proposed, Ford reminded DOL: "We are, in fact, developing a considerable body of controversy in administration of this law because of the absence of these regulations."[169]

DOL intends to continue our "enforcement efforts and our multi-media information campaign," DeLury stated, "and will get as many farm labor contractors registered as possible so that the benefits of the law will be available" to the crews.[170] Then, he turned to administration. We have "a total of 19 man-years assigned to the activities under this Act" to cover the entire country.[171] As one of the later witnesses explained, "[m]ost of our [farm] workers are Spanish-speaking people."[172] As things then stood, "... we do not have a Spanish-speaking compliance officer."[173]

MORE SPECIALIZED CONCERNS WITH FLCRA

Older questions — whether dormant or never having been formally raised —assumed a sharper focus. Since the regulations had not been released at that time, there was a good bit of speculation about almost all aspects of FLCRA.

Internal Definitions

Representative Ford, speaking at the 1975 hearings on FLCRA, suggested that "that the lack of definitions and uniform regulations" seems to be the heart of complaints. He urged that the target date for release of the regulations (then, by the end of November) be moved up "so that we can start solving these problems before everybody ends up in court?"[174] Robert Chase, Deputy Assistant Secretary of Labor, assured Ford that regulations have received "priority attention" but that it was impossible, just then, to provide "an earlier date."[175]

For ten years under the act, it was assumed that everyone understood what was meant by *a crew leader* or *farm labor contractor* or *a migrant worker*. After 1974, however, definitions became more problematic. Some witnesses asserted that they "had no objections" to the act[176] and that FLCRA was "appropriate and reasonable"[177] — so long as it was not *their clients* who were affected. "In our wildest dreams we did not consider that the people which we represent," stated industry spokesman R. V. Thornton, "would be covered" under FLCRA.[178]

Who Is a Farm Labor Contractor?

Representative McFall stated that he had received numerous inquiries concerning DOL's efforts to register a farm or ranch foreman as a farm labor contractor. Under the 1974 compromise, a foreman might be FLCRA-exempt if, *in his regular work*, he performs duties other than assisting his employer in acquiring migrant workers. But, how might one distinguish between primary and secondary duties? "Clearly," DeLury objected, "this language does not provide an exemption from the application of the law to all full-time employees."[179]

The relationship of the contractor to the grower was critical and, it would seem, difficult to define. Does the contractor provide services (employees) to one employer or to several? What services does he provide to the employees? What records does the contractor keep? Guinn Sinclair observed of California:

> We have examples of where a contractor has been successfully prosecuted, his license has been revoked by the State, and the next day he is still with the same crews working the same ranches, only now he is an employee of the ranch. Clearly he is still a farm labor contractor....[180]

Conversely, if a grower provides farm hands to a series of farmers, when does he cross the line from grower to contractor? Suddenly, such questions become relevant — and, ultimately, perhaps, a subject of litigation.

And Who is a Migrant?

How long might a migrant remain in one location before he or she ceased to be migratory? Some workers are engaged by a firm (or firms) in an area for two, three — ten months out of the year. Can a migrant also be seasonal? "They come back every year. You see ... we have county housing." "They come there and they live in those houses until the crops are over." "They are really not migrant because they only come from Texas to Patterson [California]"[181]

Another witness stated, "To my way of thinking, a migrant worker is one who travels away from his regular place of residence. A great many of these migrant workers who move throughout the United States in agricultural labor, live and make their homes in our immediate area ... ," he stated. "They come back to that area about this time of year and stay there, generally, until about May again."[182]

Representative Ford asked about the responsibility for transportation while recruiting. "The only time we ever go out and recruit anybody, we don't recruit them really, we just go down ... to Calexico. We have 23 foremen this year in cantaloups and those 23 foremen will go out."[183] This would seem to recall the initial question implied by Representative McFall: When is a foreman a regular employee and when is he really a farm labor contractor? Conversely, does it really matter so long as he or she is engaged in the work of a farm labor contractor?

Interpreting the Word "Personally"

In 1974, the concept of *personally* was added to the list of exemptions. "While this language is clear with respect to sole proprietors," DeLury stated, "interpretative problems do arise with respect to partnerships, associations, joint stock companies, trusts and corporations." DeLury explained how it might apply to an individual with the responsibility of "a sole proprietor" if he "acts personally with respect only to farm labor contracting activities at the operation involved." But, he concluded, such an interpretation may raise problems of proof to be resolved on a "case-by-case basis."[184]

Ford responded that he was "loath to suggest that his committee would ever write anything that is ambiguous," stating: "What we are really trying to do is find the point at which we should ascribe responsibility for the employer/employee relationship." Again: "The farm labor contractor that we are trying to reach is the body broker."[185]

Reaching the *body broker*, however, proved difficult. Some in agriculture objected to DOL's interpretation of *personally*: i.e., "... a farmer who operates as an individual and performs all the activity ... without the assistance of any employee, agent or contractor...."[186] But firms have "a variety of arrangements" with the grower.

> A small grower may produce a crop to the point of harvest, then through one of several arrangements, have that crop harvested by a shipper. The shipper will harvest, pack and sell the crop, based on financial arrangements with the grower. We also have large cooperatives which provide harvesting, packing, and sales facilities for its [sic] grower members.

It was asserted that, in a large company, there could be "between 10 and 30 small growers for whom some agricultural work is done by the company's employees." Obviously, it was explained, "the owner does not personally engage in such activity" but allows the duties to be "delegated."[187]

In other cases, ownership itself becomes a factor. Where crops are harvested in the field by a client (non-grower) making use of migratory labor (but, with the crops still owned by a separate entity, the grower), who is the responsible party? If ownership changes hands while the crop is in the field, does responsibility follow the crops? There seemed, suddenly, a host of issues that may not have been considered when FLCRA was largely unenforced — but, after the 1974 amendments, became critical.

On an Incidental Basis

"A full time or regular employee of a farmer is exempt," wrote Dante Nomellini, a Stockton-based attorney for the growers, if he is engaged in farm labor contracting activity for his employer "on no more than an incidental basis." The term, "'incidental' is not defined," he declared, but the "plain meaning" would seem to render him exempt if his "labor contracting function was not his primary function or primary responsibility."[188]

What was plain to Nomellini was less so to DOL. DeLury, with other Departmental witnesses, objected that the agency had received virtually no guidance from Congress. "Unfortunately," said Bobbye Spears, Associate Solicitor and charged with preparation of the regulations, "the act does not think in terms of the primary duty, nor does it tell us to look behind the subjective interest of the employer in hiring a particular person."[189]

Arguably, a case-by-case approach might have resolved the problem; but, in practice, such discretion may have been ill-advised. For example, "a farmer's or processor's operations manager, his personnel director, his foreman, or all of them, may find that they must, for a temporary period, devote an unusual amount of their time to soliciting, recruiting, or hiring workers." In the process (for a brief period), the amount of time expended might "substantially exceed" the time taken by a farm labor contractor for roughly similar tasks.[190]

'Who for a Fee ..'

Another aspect of FLCRA administration that caused concern was interpretation of *who, for a fee....* Perry Ellsworth (National Council of Agricultural Employers) argued that the term, as used under the act, had several potential meanings. A "fee" would seem to mean "a payment asked or given for a specific service." But DOL would argue that if a full-time employee "has any dealings with agricultural labor, a portion of the salary that employee receives is a 'fee.'"[191] On this matter, Representative Ford wrote to Secretary Dunlop: "... I would assume that the words 'for a fee' would not be construed to include any part of the salary of a full-time or regular employee who, as part of his job, is required to transport workers between a meeting place in the city and his employer's farm."[192]

As with many areas of labor policy, an answer may have been complex. For example, the Benita Packing Company, one of the firms in contention, "goes into the field with its own employees, harvests the crop, brings it to the packing shed, packs it for market and sells the commodity on behalf of the grower," stated attorney Donald Dressler. "*The grower pays a fee which covers the labor expense....*" Benita Packing "is in control of the workers at all times" and the "*grower has no control or involvement with them at all.*" (Italics added.) In this case, to whom would FLCRA apply — if, indeed, it would apply at all?[193]

Leon Gordon, counsel for the Agricultural Producers Labor Committee (a labor co-op serving Arizona and California), also addressed the issue of fees. The Committee is non-profit, but operates a series of worker-related activities.[194] "Its books are zeroed out at the end of the year, and each grower defrays his exact proportionate share of the cost of the labor and overhead expenses of the association determined on a volume basis." However, DOL "... has adamantly taken the position that *a fee is involved* even in the case of a cooperative labor association...." (Italics added.) The result was litigation — with Gordon drawn into court to protect the grower/co-ops.[195]

Insurance

Under FLCRA, insurance was to have been roughly on a par with common carriers used to transport passengers in interstate commerce. Several concerns were voiced here — some focusing upon the character of the farm labor contractor. [196]

The farm labor contractor "... is a small businessman. He has just one little truck that he is trying to make a living with.... If he owns two or three trucks, it is just that much more," one witness stated. "It is the recordkeeping, the details. He does not have a bookkeeper. *In most instances, he cannot read and write himself very well.*

He is being required to keep all these records that he just does not have any way of doing." "In the first place, many of them cannot afford the insurance requirements even if they can find a company that will write the insurance." Finally, he concluded, "We do not quite understand why we should be required to furnish all of these buses and all these high insurance requirements to transport people 5 or 6 miles. Many of our workers are not transported more than just 10 or 15 or 20 miles."[197]

Bobbye Spears, with the Solicitor's Office, addressed the same issue — but with a somewhat different twist. She recalled a recent case in which a farmer said that "I have to have peas picked tomorrow and a neighbor farmer saying, I will be glad to round up a crew of people and transport them down to your farm and pick your peas tomorrow." Ms. Spears noted: "The helpful farmer took his truck, which, in this case, was an open truck, transported them down to the neighbor's farm, they picked the peas, and on the way back there was a wreck. There were several children under the age of 12. I believe that three were killed."[198]

EMPLOYMENT OF ALIENS

"Quite obviously, we anticipated that a central problem in dealing with this law would be the problem of illegal aliens," stated Representative Ford, "because it was one of the purposes we had in mind in amended the law."[199] Several factors were at issue: the bureaucracy, employer-employee relations, and the local reaction.

Dealing with the Bureaucracy

Warren Landis of the Wage/Hour Division affirmed that DOL had "worked very closely with ... Immigration and Naturalization" but suggested the issue was "quite thorny." Landis speculated,

> What, in fact, constitutes *knowing employment* of illegal aliens and what are the bona-fide efforts that a contractor would make so that he would be absolved of knowing employment of illegal aliens? (Italics added.)
>
> I wish we had a full answer this morning, but we do not. This is another situation that we are addressing on a case-by-case basis.

Landis stated that he had "one case where we denied a certificate ... because of a history of employment of illegal aliens" and we have "some other — perhaps similar — cases that are pending." John Silver of the Wage/Hour Division from Fresno noted that "... the Border Patrol indicates to us that they believe that 30 percent of the farmworkers who are harvesting crops in California are illegal aliens. So," he stated, "... you can see that our problems are great." Part of the problem may have been linguistic. "There are groups where very few of them speak English. They cannot communicate," observed Joe Fernandez, with the Wage/Hour Division from Raleigh, North Carolina, and "we have had difficulty locating a crew leader."[200]

Ford turned to Bobbye Spears of the Solicitor's Office. Do the contemplated regulations have "any specific requirements" to show that a grower or farm labor contractor actually "tried to know" the worker's status? Spears replied, "We have been working very closely with the INS lawyers and with the Attorney General's staff to see what would be reasonable within constitutional restraints." She added, "What could we require within the constraints of the Constitution? What sort of affirmative duty could we place on the grower?" Spears stated, "We think we have a reasonable set of requirements which we do intend to propose when the regulations come out." But, she added: "It is very tricky."[201]

Reaction from the Industry

"The burden placed ... on the employer," stated Dante Nomellini, attorney for the growers, "to be able to identify an illegal alien" is "unfair and in most cases the labor contractor or the farmer or any employer is not in a position to accomplish an adequate interrogation of the individual involved."[202]

Nomellini acknowledged that the statute says "knowingly," but that the act still placed an unfair burden upon the employer. An illegal, picked up and deported, may end up back on the same farm — without the employer-grower being aware.

> You have to recognize that the farmer himself is not just one individual working on the farm and he is not the one who goes out and supervises the worker and he is not the one generally who has the contact. We have a language differential here ... most of the farmers are not fluent in Spanish nor are they capable, or their agents, of interrogating that man to find out if he is legal or illegal without violating that man's rights.

He suggested, after analysis, that it can be asked "if he is a lawful resident of the United States" and for "his name and social security number." "We don't have this capability to interrogate. The Border Patrol, a very sophisticated group of people who have been trained, even they have problems. The burden shouldn't be placed on industry."[203]

Nomellini's solution was direct. The State Department "ought to be asked to cooperate with Congress in coming up with a situation where the individual who is an illegal, once apprehended, is punished in a significant way so that ... he won't come back across the border." The problem, he stated, "has to be attacked at its roots and that is right at the border. If anything significant is going to be done to keep aliens out — *and I don't know whether we want to*, that's a matter of policy...." (Italics added.) It's a matter for the Congress and for those directly involved: "... not the farmers and not the labor contractors and not the general employers in industry."[204]

The Local Reaction

Scott Toothaker, a management attorney from Texas, lives right up against the Mexican border. And, that creates another dimension to the problem. Some Spanish-speakers may be illegal — but others may be local.

> How is this truck driver [picking up job applicants] with nothing more than a second, third, fourth, or fifth grade education, to pass on whether that guy is an illegal alien or not? They all have some kind of a card.... But I defy anyone in this [hearing] room to tell me whether he is an illegal alien.

Ford responded that regulations — which "have not yet been written" — provide ways through which to render an analysis. The presumption of knowingly employing an alien "would have to be overcome by proving actual knowledge, and while it is less than perfect, we do know that there are ... people who habitually rehire people."[205]

Guinn Sinclair, representative of the farm labor contractors, voiced similar concerns, suggesting that "the Department of State should be the one" to determine who is in the country illegally. "Trying to get the businessman to enforce the laws of the United States just is not good."[206]

Zora Arredondo was equally direct. A self-described "hillbilly from Kentucky talking before all these lawyers," queried: "Do you know what it is to need to have your crops thinned, or weeded before you can irrigate and you have 1 or 2 days before you get the water? Have you ever seen fruit that was falling on the ground ready to be picked?" Moving on to policy implications:

> If you need people and some come to the field wanting to work, you are going to put them to work. The crop is the important thing, not who the man is or where he comes from. Besides, the place to stop the illegal aliens isn't there in the fields, it is at the port of entry. (...) Do we have the right to ask people if they are citizens? The Department of Labor doesn't know the answer.

Ms. Arredondo turned to the Members: "Do you? When we do ask people for papers, they tell you, 'I don't have to show you my papers.' How many of us have anything to prove we are U.S. citizens? I don't."[207]

NEW REGULATIONS RELEASED

On June 29, 1976, final regulations were published. Of 61 substantive comments, items of principal concern were (a) the increased amounts of insurance coverage, (b) the applicability of the amended act to include intrastate, as well as interstate, farm labor activities, and (c) the proposed regulations relating to illegal aliens.[208]

On insurance coverage, DOL "concluded that the increased amounts ... were necessary to protect workers." Coverage of intrastate farm workers was, of course, part of the 1974 Act and could not be changed without legislation.[209] Concerning employment of aliens, the farm labor contractor was to give evidence of "an affirmative showing of a bona fide inquiry of each prospective employee's status as a United States citizen or as a person lawfully authorized to work in the United States." The regulation provides a series of acceptable routes — birth certificate, certificate of naturalization, passport, certain INS forms — through which a determination might be made.[210]

COVERAGE AND CONTROVERSY

With the passage of time, some Members of Congress, with others, began to reassess the impact of FLCRA and to urge modification of coverage. At least three areas stand out: custom combining, poultry harvesting, and detasseling of corn.

Custom Combining, Hay Harvesting, and Sheep Shearing

On March 4, 1976, Representative Larry Pressler (R-SD) introduced legislation to exempt from FLCRA "contractors of workers engaged in custom cutting or combine operations" and "contractors of workers engaged in the shearing of sheep."[211] Roughly comparable legislation was introduced on March 9 with two more bills on March 11.[212]

"In Nebraska, the major part of our extensive wheat acreage is harvested by 'custom cutters,'" stated Representative Virginia Smith (R-NE). "These operations do not involve migrant labor in the accepted sense of the definition," she stated, "... so all of the added precaution against abuses is not necessary." Smith suggested that these contractors and crew leaders "... should not be required to be registered, or to be certified, or to meet the other requirements for insurance, transportation, and housing." Seeking exemption, she stated: "Otherwise, we have placed a hardship on the agricultural equivalent of the small businessman and ... have subjected him to more of that over-regulation which strangles and can eventually destroy."[213]

Members from other grain growing states also suggested change. James Abourezk (D-SD) introduced a new bill (March 18), observing that the 1974 FLCRA amendments had "inadvertently expanded the scope of the law to cover sheep shearers and custom combine crews." Senators Lloyd Bentsen (D-TX) and Abourezk had met with Department officials on the issue; Senator Nelson and Representative Ford had written to DOL. These informal efforts, however, were of no avail.[214]

Senator Robert Dole (R-KS) explained the purposes of the exemption. FLCRA was intended "to end abuses against migrant workers and farmers" by farm labor contractors. While custom combining workers are migratory (starting in Texas and moving on to the far north), they were really not migratory in the sense that farm laborers might be. There was "no record of exploiting or abusing" of such employees. As for safety and health requirements, "custom operators are already meeting the standards necessary to protect their employees." Thus, Senator Dole saw "no need for the additional safety and health requirements" of FLCRA. He objected to "time-consuming paperwork" and to requirements for "higher insurance. FLCRA was intended for farmworkers "from a poverty-stricken environment," who have "little or no knowledge of the English language," and are moved in "unsafe transportation." Dole concluded, "There is no similarity in any respect between farm labor contractors and custom combine operators"[215] — or sheep shearing crews, for that matter.

On March 23, Representative Pressler introduced yet another version of his FLCRA-exemption bill — as did Representative Berkeley Bedell (D-IA).[216] Bedell had written to the Department on February 23, 1976, and, his request for exemption having been denied, he called DOL and spoke with Herbert Cohen of Wage/Hour. Cohen acknowledged receiving communications from Members involved in drafting the act.

> He [Cohen] then related that, despite this testimony, the Department decided to proceed with the implementation of the new requirements because its lawyers felt that the legislative history of the 1974 amendments did not specifically call for the exemption of such crews.[217]

Bedell called the incident "a classic example of the executive branch using its rulemaking authority to usurp the legislative function of the Congress" and of "attempting to legislate by fiat." Finally, he called upon the Congress "to thwart executive excesses in the rulemaking area" by enacting corrective legislation.[218]

On March 23, as the Senate considered the Rural Development Act of 1972, Senator Dole proposed FLCRA exemption of custom combine, hay harvesting, and sheep shearing workers. Senators Abourezk, Bentsen, and Nelson were supportive; without dissent, the amendment was adopted.[219] The following day, Representative Tom Foley, a Democrat from Washington state, called up the Rural Development Act with the Dole amendment. Mr. Foley explained that the problem was "technical" —that the issues were neither "labor contractors [n]or migrant laborers" but, rather, "independent contractors who until now have not been subjected" to the FLCRA.[220] The only other speaker was Representative Ford — who announced that, although the subject matter of the bill should have been directed to a subcommittee of the Committee on Education and Labor, he would not object.[221]

On April 5, 1976, the Rural Development Act (with the Dole amendment) was signed into law (P.L. 94-259).[222]

Poultry Services

During the spring of 1976, a seemingly uncontroversial bill was introduced dealing with internal Department of Agriculture administration. The measure was passed by the House[223] and was forwarded to the Senate. There, it was reported on September 30, 1976, considered later that same day, and passed with an amendment.[224]

Referred back to the House, Representative Tom Foley presented the measure and the clerk read the title of the bill and the Senate amendments. At the conclusion, a paragraph had been added amending FLCRA.

> (9) any custom poultry harvesting, breeding, debeaking, sexing, or health service operation, providing the employees of the operation are not regularly required to be away from their domicile other than during their normal working hours.

Representative Edward Madigan (R-IL) queried: "I wonder if the gentleman ... could explain the one amendment the Senate has placed on the bill." Foley responded: "...the Senate has placed on the bill a provision relating to the Farm Labor Contractor Registration Act." William Wampler (R-VA) added that the FLCRA amendment was the only change in the House-passed bill.[225]

The bill was approved, sent to the White House and signed into law on October 1976 (P.L. 94-561).

To Detassel and Rogue Hybrid Seed Corn

During hearings early in 1978, Representative Virginia Smith complained about the "narrowminded and ridiculous interpretations" of the "over-zealous bureaucrats at the Department of Labor who don't have anything better to do than harass our businessmen." Smith went on to discuss actions that "endanger yet another of the fragile freedoms that still exist for individuals in this country."[226] She observed that "thousands of farmers" have "come to Washington during the past few weeks in search of help to raise farm prices." To raise farm income, she seemed to suggest, farmers should be permitted to pay less to the "several thousand high school students" who are hired each year "to detassel seed corn, thin out test plots or rogue sorghum." She stated,

> ... in no way can the salary from this job be considered as their primary means of support. In many cases, it is more of a social event than a job. It also provides a good opportunity for a coach, high school teacher, or college student to pick up some extra money and for the students to keep in touch during part of the summer.

Ms. Smith stated, "I believe that unless this law is changed to stop the action proposed by the Department of Labor, we face a serious challenge to our freedom."[227]

On April 11, Representative James Leach (R-IA) introduced H.Res. 1124 expressing the sense of the House "that certain individuals employed in the detasseling of hybrid seed corn should not be considered to be migrant workers" for purposes of FLCRA.[228] Shortly thereafter, a bill was introduced by Leach that would have amended FLCRA to deal with the same issue.[229] No hearings were held: in legislative terms, the issue seemed to disappear. Momentum, however, was building.

In September, the "Perishable Agricultural Commodities Act" (PACA) was under consideration. Senator Richard Clark (D-IA) proposed an amendment to FLCRA to correct "an example of government out of control." The amendment would exempt "a portion of the seed industry" from FLCRA registration. "These are young people [with about 280,000 young persons who work seasonally] ranging in age from 14 to 16 years old who work for an average of 10 days to 2 weeks each summer," Clark stated, and who "detassel seed corn, eliminate 'rogue' plants, and perform other functions, related to seed production." The employees are from the local area, residing within a 30 to 40 mile radius, and who return to their home each evening, he suggested. These people are "clearly not migrants by any reasonable definition."[230] His constituents "are very much up in arms about this," he stated, "and ... I do not blame them."[231]

It had only been through the past year, it was stated, that DOL had sought to enforce FLCRA against the seed corn industry.[232] On February 23, 1978, Senator Clark had addressed a letter to Secretary Marshall in which the issue was discussed and followed that up with a phone call to Marshall and a personal visit with Assistant Secretary Daniel Elisburg, but

DOL "refused to change its position."[233] Senator Richard Lugar (R-IN) similarly wrote to Marshall in late July, but without apparent impact.[234] Now, with no objection having been heard, an amendment was added to PACA and a quarter-plus million workers were exempted from FLCRA.

The Clark amendment was accepted and approved by the Congress.[235] On November 1, 1978, the root bill was signed into law (P.L. 95-562).

THE LESSENING COVERAGE OF FLCRA

Various segments of the agricultural industry had been eliminated from FLCRA coverage as, it was argued, the wrong people were brought under the act's purview. Senator David Boren (D-OK) would later observe: "We could go through the entire food and fiber industry, sector by sector, adopting amendments to clarify the act." He suggested that a wiser course would be to "enact legislation to clarify the act completely once and for all."[236]

Hearings in the House: 1978

In mid-1977, Representative McFall wrote once more to Secretary Marshall concerning registration under FLCRA. McFall stated that farmers in his district (part of the San Joaquin Valley) would be forced to register as farm labor contractors under the definition of *personally*.[237] Marshall's response was less than some Members had hoped, providing the context for the 1978 hearings.[238]

Starting from the McFall/Marshall correspondence, the hearings explored a variety of FLCRA definitions. Most critics followed the lead of Perry Ellsworth (National Council of Agricultural Employers). He did not seek to diminish worker protections, but, that having been said, he continued to argue against the "untold harassment" of farmers and others — who were "by no stretch of the imagination crew leaders."[239] Many argued for the original intent of Congress.[240]

Day haul workers raised broader questions. Representative William Hefner (D-NC) acknowledged that such workers had not been "inadvertently included under the law." Still, he urged the Members to "reexamine those intentions" and to exempt workers living within a 75-mile radius of agricultural operations. "In North Carolina," he stated, "day haul workers are almost always, local, permanent residents of the area in which they work." They do not necessarily go through a labor contractor and, when they do, "... it is more a matter of convenience rather than economic necessity." He stated: "Day haul workers *are not migrant workers, as the term is commonly understood*.... And day haul operators, who transport these workers ... are not crew leaders in the usual sense of this term."[241] (Italics added.)

But, if not migratory, such workers may still have been subject to transportation provided by growers or contractors. "The gist of this problem seems to be in the insurance coverage required of anyone defined by the law as a farm labor contractor, whether he transports local day labor or true migrant labor," Hefner stated. No one suggests that day haul workers go unprotected, he stated, but they still have under state insurance laws requirements similar to "all other workers in the State."[242]

The issue was taken up by Representative B. F. Sisk (D-CA) in a letter to DOL. Elisburg replied that state coverage varied "in accordance with the mandate of the particular state legislation." Such laws are work-related and apply only where "the passengers are clearly 'employees' of the insured employer." Dependents of migrant workers are not covered, Elisburg continued. "In addition, liability under State workers compensation plans would not extend to the times migrant workers are being transported from one employer to a prospective employer."[243]

These several issues were joined with respect to shared worker arrangements. Representative David Stockman (R-MI) proposed that FLCRA should not apply to farmers who shared the services of agricultural workers and who receive "no monetary consideration" other than actual expenses. "The potential for abuse," Representative Stockman stated, "is in my view almost nil."[244] Elisburg responded that, "as an enforcement policy," DOL "would prefer to put our resources elsewhere" rather than come after small farmers who, on a local basis, share workers.[245] The response did not satisfy Stockman, and Representative William Goodling (R-PA) suggested: "He [Elisburg] is saying if we had more resources we would get after them, too...." But Elisburg stated, "... large or small, if we found abuses of the work force we would go wherever they are."[246]

Some urged that legislation exempt "nonprofit charitable organizations," "public or nonprofit private educational institutions," and "bona fide nonprofit agricultural cooperatives engaged in labor contracting for their own members." Elisburg suggested that such proposals were something of a ruse — and one that DOL would oppose — that they would "substantially narrow the act's coverage and would deny its protection to large numbers of agricultural workers." Elisburg stated,

We have been told by those who support this exemption that such organizations are fixed and have assets which would be reachable in a law suit by their employees. I think that we all have to recognize, generally, agricultural workers do not have the financial resources to independently assert their rights against such organizations, and we question why this economically disadvantaged group should be placed in this position.

Further, Elisburg stated that "... employment by a nonprofit organization has nothing to do with a need to protect agricultural workers under FLCRA, particularly if the nonprofit venture consists of profit-making organizations."[247]

Concerns Grow

"These individuals," registered under FLCRA, are "not farmers; they were 'agents' who arranged to provide migrant labor to farmers," Representative Stockman affirmed. Many of them have "long criminal records. They stole from the workers, they stole from the farmers, and they needlessly endangered the health and safety of migrant workers."[248]

Yet, it was with these same, perhaps unscrupulous, middlemen that farmers dealt. The contractors, some alleged, provided the services of low-wage and, often low-skilled workers: some Native Americans, some foreign-born — and some ineligible to work in the United States. They broke strikes, some said, and prevented domestic workers from organizing. Further, critics suggested that they provided cover for their farmer/business partners.

DOL, some urged, had "consistently misinterpreted" the rules governing such contractors. Though he believed "that agricultural workers must be protected from abuse by unethical crew leaders" (a consistent sub-theme of FLCRA critics), Representative Leon Panetta (D-CA) protested that "family farmers" were "forced to comply with complicated registration forms, maintain detailed records, and are subject to a variety of investigations and inspections." Faced with "growing anger" from the farming community, Representative Panetta proposed a substantial restructuring of FLCRA.[249]

Relations with the Department of Labor

Under date of October 24, 1979, fifty-two Senators [led by J. Bennett Johnston (D-LA)] wrote to Secretary Marshall expressing "our increasing concern" over DOL's management of FLCRA.

The Johnston letter explained the purposes of the act (as the signers perceived them) and observed that "farmers and certain other agricultural employers" are being required to register — "a requirement we believe goes beyond any reasonable interpretation of the law." DOL's actions, "apparently based on its own extremely narrow interpretation" of the act, are "completely contrary to Congressional intent," and impose "an undue penalty and economic burden on those specifically exempted" by Congress. "... these actions have resulted in a misdirection of the Department's limited resources at the expense of those the law was intended to protect."[250]

Marshall's response, dated November 26, 1979, offered few accommodations. He agreed that enforcement of the act "be targeted on repeat and serious violations which jeopardize labor standards...." Marshall observed that the first ten years "under the Act" have not ended abuse. Thus, the 1974 amendments were enacted "to extend coverage and improve enforcement."

The Secretary acknowledged that a farmer (or other agriculturally-related person) would be exempt if he or she "'personally' recruited migrant labor for their own operation" and that "any full-time or regular employees of any incorporated farm or agricultural business" might also be exempt if the employee "only performed farm labor contractor-type activities on an 'incidental' basis." On both issues, DOL had been consistent.

> We believe ... that FLCRA applies where there is a crewleader hiring or transporting workers or where there are company employees substantially engaged in activities generally performed by crewleaders. We also believe that it is critical to enforce the Act in a way which discourages evasion of its provisions — *to deter farm labor contractors from being placed on payrolls and appearing to assume the status of full-time or regular employees.* This enforcement approach is consistent with both the letter and spirit of the Act. (Italics added.)

The Secretary conceded that "the term 'incidental'" may not have been defined "as specifically as possible." He therefore stated that, for the future, such a person would be one "who does not spend more than 20 percent of his time in farm labor contracting activities and performs that activity solely for his employer." These changes will provide "clarity [to] our enforcement position while at the same time preserving important protections for farm workers under the Act."[251]

The Senators were not entirely pleased with Marshall's letter. On December 5, 1979, Senator Johnston [with Russell Long (D-LA)] concurred with Marshall's emphasis on "'traditional farm labor contractors'" — and

requested "a copy of instructions being prepared for enforcement officers."
But, they disagreed on the impact of such changes.

> First, in order to know if an employee is engaged on more than an
> incidental basis, he must be engaged less than 20 percent of some time
> period. Logically, the time period should be his total manhours of
> employment. The failure of your letter to specify a time period leaves open
> the possibility that '20 percent of his time' means 20 percent of any work
> week, any work day, or any pay period. Any one of these possible
> meanings would render the 20 percent standard ineffective as far as
> strengthening the exemption provided by Congress.

> Second, your letter is not specific about the meaning of farm labor
> contracting activities. As we understand the Department's interpretation of
> the Act, supervision is considered to be a farm labor contracting activity.
> Since your letter does not clarify this, the new definition of 'incidental'
> again becomes less significant.

> Third, your letter does not indicate what regulatory standing the new
> definition of 'incidental' would have. The Department's intent should have
> been set forth in formal regulations, subject to public comment. Similarly,
> the interpretative regulations for the Act itself are long overdue.[252]

Through the last year and a half that Marshall was in office, such
correspondence took on a regular pattern as first one and then another
Member of Congress became distressed with the provisions of FLCRA.

The Boren Amendment and the Panetta Bill (1980)

During consideration of the Child Nutrition Amendments of 1980,
Senator Boren proposed an amendment "to clarify the provisions" of
FLCRA. "All of us," he commenced, "... want to see an end to any abuse of
migrant farm workers. But, at the same time," he affirmed, "We very
strongly want to assure that an additional regulatory burden is not placed
upon the farmers, the farm co-ops, and others involving agriculture across
the country."[253]

Senator Boren was critical of DOL administration of FLCRA. It had
moved, he stated, "far from the intent of the Congress" and of those who
spoke on the 1963 legislation. The Department has been "subjecting farmers
and other agricultural employers, including their employees, to civil and
criminal penalties for failing to comply with" the requirements of the act.
Senator Boren listed organizations that had "joined in support" of his

amendment. He called upon DOL "to quit harassing the farmers" and "to curb ... unnecessary abuse of authority by the bureaucracy.[254]

The Senate was split. Senator Gaylord Nelson noted that the bill was essentially similar to S. 2875, introduced with 39 cosponsors a month earlier. Nelson urged that Boren, having made his point, would "be willing to withdraw his amendment" and to wait for hearings that had already been scheduled by his (Nelson's) Committee. "As the Senator knows, this law is within the exclusive jurisdiction of the Labor and Human Resources Committee." There was yet another option: i.e., S. 2789, introduced by Senator Javits. Senator Nelson agreed that there have been "serious problems" since enactment of the 1974 amendments. "Numerous lawsuits have been filed, and both agricultural employers as well as farm workers have expressed dissatisfaction" with DOL's administration of this law — "and justifiably so, in my opinion." Senator Nelson noted that he had personally written to the Secretary "expressing my concern." But, he also affirmed that the proper place for consideration of "corrective legislation" was the Labor and Human Resources Committee.[255]

The Boren amendment, however, was not withdrawn and, on a vote of 57 yeas to 37 nays, the measure was passed.[256]

The House was similarly divided on the issue. Representative Panetta, who had earlier introduced general reform of FLCRA, was now joined by Representatives Foley (of Washington State, chair of the Agriculture Committee) and William Goodling of the Committee on Education and Labor, with numerous others.[257] Panetta affirmed,

> The Farm Labor Contractor Registration Act was passed in 1963 to protect migrant farmworkers from abuse by unscrupulous crew leaders. This act was also intended to protect farmers and other agricultural employers from the irresponsible action of some crew leaders. I firmly believe that the act should continue to serve that purpose.[258]

But it may need a few changes. "Unfortunately, in spite of the request of a majority of the Senate, the problem has not been resolved," Representative Panetta observed, noting "misinterpretations by the Department," "ambiguities in the act," and "a particular interpretation of its statutory authority."[259] Representative Goodling (with John Ashbrook (R-OH), ranking Member on the Committee on Education and Labor) offered an amendment "to clarify the act." DOL, Goodling stated, has engaged in "unnecessary and unproductive harassment" of many Pennsylvania farmers.[260]

In early September, Representative Goodling again addressed the House. His amendments, he said, "except for technical improvements," basically parallel the Panetta and Boren proposals — which he urged his colleagues to support.[261] Goodling was not alone: "over 100 Members of the House" (including Panetta) endorsed the Boren option.[262] Representative Ford did not. "I strongly oppose the Boren amendment," he stated. "... it would effectively repeal the FLCRA, the only Federal legislation that protects migrant farmworkers against the most common abuses they endure in their hiring, transportation, housing, and employment in agricultural labor." Ford placed in the *Record* a letter from Ray Marshall in which he, too, expressed "my deep concern and strong opposition" to the Boren amendment."[263]

The Boren amendment, however, was caught up in parliamentary procedures and migrated to a series of proposals. In a report for 1980, the *CQ Almanac* noted: "An amendment restricting coverage of a 1963 law aimed at preventing exploitation of migrant farm workers was added to a continuing resolution (H.J.Res. 637) but later dropped."[264] For the present, FLCRA remained unchanged.

The Boren Bill and the Panetta Bill (1981)

In the 97th Congress, critics of the Farm Labor Contractor Registration Act returned to the fray. On April 8, 1981, Senator Boren introduced S. 922, a measure designed "to provide for the proper administration and enforcement of" FLCRA. Conceding that one problem has been the "somewhat vague and ambiguous" language that had "resulted in gross misinterpretation," Boren's proposal sought "to clarify" the meaning of the act.[265]

Senator Chiles, co-sponsor of the Boren bill, having "stressed my support" for the purposes of the act, stated that FLCRA's "vague language and convoluted format" allows DOL to "subvert ... the intent of Congress" and to take advantage "of these procedural defects in its unrelenting efforts to envelop farmers, packers, processors, and their employees within the regulatory scheme of the act." The result has been "widespread harassment" of agricultural interests with "little discernable effect" with respect to crew leaders. Farmers "face enough problems in today's economy without this one."[266]

On May 20, 1981, Representative Panetta introduced H.R. 3636, similar in some respects to his bill from the 96th Congress.[267] FLCRA remains, he stated, "a significant problem of unnecessary and burdensome regulation" which has "grown as more and more farmers and other fixed-base agricultural employers" have found that they are required to comply with its terms.[268]

In the interim between introduction of the Boren bill and Panetta bill, however, there had been a discernible change. The Education and Labor Committee, Representative Panetta announced, "is contemplating hearings" on the issue this year, and there is "no doubt in my mind that we can work out the problems that exist with the act." Panetta wrote into his bill several proposals which may have been viewed as the start of compromise. *First*: He proposed to eliminate the "distinction between 'full-time or regular'" and to make clear the distinction between "a bona fide employee and an independent contractor." *Second*: He proposed to allow the Secretary some discretion in causing "a cooperative to register," depending upon the purposes of the co-operative arrangement. *Third*: He proposed a modification in the definition of "day-haul worker" with the stated intention of securing their protection.[269]

"It is in this constructive spirit," Panetta affirmed, "that I look forward to working with my colleagues on the Committee on Education and Labor, and particularly with my good friend from California (Mr. Miller), who is chairman of the Subcommittee on Labor Standards."[270] But, negotiations would be long and intense.

The Miller Hearings and Their Aftermath (1982)

From the spring of 1981 and into the fall of 1982, the several parties at interest met and reviewed proposals for revision of FLCRA. From all sides, there were serious concerns "with the existing law that they felt needed to be addressed," according to Representative George Miller. Negotiations, he stated, "were long and, at times, frustrating."[271] Finally, on September 1, 1982, Secretary of Labor Raymond Donovan sent to Congress a bill entitled the "Migrant and Seasonal Agricultural Worker Protection Act which was referred to the Committee on Education and Labor."[272]

The Hearing

On September 14, 1982, Miller called together for a single hearing the Subcommittee on Labor Standards. The bill at issue was H.R. 7102, an Administration proposal but with more generalized backing. Robert B. Collyer, Deputy Under Secretary of Labor, was the first witness. Reviewing the recent history of the Administration's bill, Collyer affirmed,

This cooperative effort has now resulted in a consensus bill, endorsed by the AFL-CIO, the migrant legal action program, and by major agricultural employer organizations, such as the American Farm Bureau Federation, the National Food Processors Association, and the National Council of Agricultural Employers.

While none of these groups believes the bill to be ideal from its individual standpoint, there is important agreement that the bill materially improves the law.[273]

The 1974 FLCRA amendments, Collyer explained, had resulted in "a great deal of litigation."[274] The essence of the new bill was compromise.

Representatives from industry and the AFL-CIO endorsed the changes in policy included within the new bill.[275] Representatives of farmworkers were more skeptical, but acquiesced.[276] As the hearing closed, Representative Miller thanked the witnesses for their support. "I take a great deal of pride in seeing that I am not the victim of testimony 5 years down the road, that it didn't work." Miller stated: "... I do recognize that a good number of your associates and clients are very skeptical about entering into this agreement." Again: "I don't know if this law is perfect or not. I think it's an improvement, and I gather from your testimony that you believe it is an improvement."[277]

Consideration and Floor Action

"The failure of current law to achieve its goal of fairness and equity for migrant workers," the House report stated, "combined with employer objections as to their treatment under the Act" gave the negotiations momentum and "made the attainment of legislative change obligatory."[278] FLCRA as amended, had "failed to reverse the historical pattern of abuse and exploitation of migrant and seasonal farm workers" and, as a result, argued for a "new approach."[279] The Committee on Education and Labor reported the bill on September 28, 1982.[280]

On September 29, Representative Miller urged that the rules be suspended and H.R. 7102 be passed. Recounting the "months of negotiations and compromise," he noted the certainty that the legislation might bring.[281] John Erlenborn (R-IL), a cosponsor, recalled that "for over 18 months the interested parties, including staff from the House and Senate majority and minority, have been engaged in negotiations" to work out a successor to FLCRA. Representative Panetta affirmed that the bill "eliminates undue red-tape and harassment for farmers ... while at the same time provides real protection to migrant and seasonal agricultural workers."

Representative Goodling, for his part, cited the "unwarranted and overzealous tactics of the wage and hour division"but, at the same time, he acknowledged that the "long negotiations between all parties" had made the new bill possible. Finally, the debate closed. The rules were suspended: the bill was passed — on a voice vote.[282

In the Senate, the bill was held at the desk (not referred to a committee)[283] until on December 19, 1982, Senator Howard Baker (R-TN) called up the measure for floor action. Senator Orrin Hatch (R-UH) remarked that the measure, now passed by the House, was "identical to the measure" that he had introduced in the Senate (S. 2930) — with Senators Boren and Edward Kennedy (D-Ma), among others, as co-sponsors. Senator Hatch reviewed the history of FLCRA and presented an analysis of H.R. 7102. As in the House, the bill was adopted by a voice vote.[284]

On January 14, 1983, H.R. 7102 was signed into law by President Ronald Reagan (P.L. 97-470). The new law "will result in substantially improved protection for migrant and seasonal agricultural workers," he said, "many of whom are disadvantaged minorities." Conversely: "We will continue our efforts to both reduce unnecessary regulatory burdens and at the same time, protect essential employment standards in America's workplaces."[285]

Chapter 5

A NEW STATUTE EMERGES (1983 FF.)

With enactment of P.L. 97-470, FLCRA disappeared. In its place was a new statute: the Migrant and Seasonal Agricultural Workers Protection Act (MSPA). For more than twenty years, MSPA has been generally (though not entirely) free from controversy.

THE STRUCTURE AND PROVISIONS OF THE NEW LAW

MSPA has remained largely unchanged since its enactment.[286] Although its terms are spelled out in detail adapted to specific farmworker employment situations, its structure is relatively simple.

The introduction states the purposes of the act: i.e., to require that farm labor contractors register with the Secretary of Labor and to assure "necessary protections for migrant and seasonal agricultural workers, agricultural associations, and agricultural employers." It then proceeds to a list of definitions used: *inter alia*, "agricultural association," "agricultural employer," "agricultural employment," "day-haul operation," "employ," "farm labor contracting activity," "farm labor contractor," "migrant agricultural worker," "person," and "seasonal agricultural worker."[287]

The act includes exemptions — i.e., some family farms and related agricultural industries. Also exempt are labor organizations, any "nonprofit charitable organization or public or private nonprofit educational institution," and any person "engaged in any farm labor contracting activity solely within a twenty-five mile interstate radius of such person's permanent place of residence and for not more than thirteen weeks per year." Custom combining, hay harvesting, or sheep shearing operations are exempt, as are persons engaged in custom poultry harvesting, breeding, debeaking, etc., where workers are not required to be away from their permanent place of residence overnight. Persons are exempt when their "principal occupation ... is not agricultural employment" and who provide "full-time students" to detassel corn, etc., when such students are not required to be away from their permanent place of residence overnight. Any "common carrier" who would be a farm labor contractor solely because the carrier is engaged in transporting migrant or seasonal agricultural workers is exempt.

Title 1 explains the conditions under which farm labor contractors are required to register and the process of registration. The registrant must be of good character (specified in the act), with right to appeal if he or she is denied registration. A certificate of registration may not be transferred or assigned and will normally cover a twelve-month period. Any change of address (or other material variation in registration) must be made known to the Secretary. Finally, the farm labor contractor is restricted from hiring aliens not authorized to work in the United States.

> (a) No farm labor contractor shall recruit, hire, employ, or use, with knowledge, the services of any individual who is an alien not lawfully admitted for permanent residence or who has not been authorized by the Attorney General to accept employment.

> "(b) A farm labor contractor shall be considered to have complied with subsection (a) if the farm labor contractor demonstrates that the farm labor contractor relied in good faith on documentation prescribed by the Secretary, and the farm labor contractor had no reason to believe the individual was an alien referred to in subsection (a).[288]

Title II deals with *migrant agricultural workers*.[289] Each "farm labor contractor, agricultural employer, and agricultural association" who employs a migrant agricultural worker shall disclose to the worker at the time of his or her recruitment: the place of employment, the wage rates to be paid, the crops and kinds of activities on which the worker may be employed, the period of employment, matters with respect to housing, transportation, and "any other employee benefit to be provided, if any," and "any costs to be charged for each of them." The existence "of any strike or other concerted work stoppage, slowdown, or interruption of operations by employees at the place of employment" must be disclosed. Any commission arrangements must also be disclosed. At each place of employment, in a conspicuous place, a form from the Secretary "setting forth the rights and protections afforded" to such migrant workers must be posted. Where housing is provided, the terms and conditions under which such housing is made available shall be provided to the migrant worker.

Each "farm labor contractor, agricultural employer, and agricultural association" who employs migrant workers shall keep specified records of his or her employment — and shall provide a copy to the migrant. The basic information (terms and conditions of employment) shall be provided in English "or, as necessary and reasonable, in Spanish or other language common to migrant agricultural workers who are not fluent or literate in English."[290] No company store arrangement is permissible.

Title III deals with *seasonal agricultural worker* protections.[291] Each "farm labor contractor, agricultural employer, and agricultural association" who recruits seasonal agricultural workers shall ascertain "and, upon request, disclose in writing," the following: the place of employment, the wage rates to be paid, the crops and kinds of activities on which the worker may be employed, the period of employment, and the costs and terms of transportation. If there is a "strike or other concerted work stoppage, slowdown, or interruption of operations," such information shall be made known. Any commission arrangement or day-haul operation shall also be made known. The various protections shall be posted in a conspicuous place.

Records will be kept with respect to an individual worker and a copy will be provided to such worker. Information to be provided will be in English or, as reasonable, "in Spanish or other language common to seasonal agricultural workers who are not fluent or literate in English."[292] Wages are to be paid "when due." There will be no company store arrangement.

Title IV deals with *further protections for migrant and seasonal agricultural workers.* The title deals primarily with insurance.[293] It begins by specifying the type/mode of transportation in question.

> This section *does not apply* [italics added] to the transportation of any migrant or seasonal agricultural worker on a tractor, combine, harvester, picker, or other similar machinery and equipment while such worker is actually engaged in the planting, cultivating, or harvesting of any agricultural commodity or the care of livestock or poultry.

However, where this section does apply (to normal and/or regular vehicle usage), the "agricultural employer, agricultural association, and farm labor contractor" shall "ensure that the vehicle does comply" with "Federal and State safety standards," and ensure that "each driver has a valid and appropriate license." Such employer shall have in effect "an insurance policy or a liability bond" that insures the employer "against liability for damage to persons or property arising from the ownership, operation, or the causing to be operated, of any vehicle used to transport any migrant or seasonal agricultural worker." The provision goes on to explain the various terms and conditions under which insurance may be applicable.

How might the individual employer confirm that the individual farm labor contractor has, indeed, complied with the terms of his or her craft?

> No person shall utilize the services of any farm labor contractor to supply any migrant or seasonal agricultural worker unless the person first takes reasonable steps to determine that the farm labor contractor possesses a certificate of registration which is valid and which authorizes the activity for which the contractor is utilized. In making that determination, the person may rely upon either possession of a certificate or registration, or confirmation of such registration by the Department of Labor. The Secretary shall maintain a central public registry of all persons issued a certificate of registration.

Title V, at the close of the act, provides for *general provisions*. These are divided into three sections and, appear, in part, as follows.

Enforcement Provisions. Any person "who willfully and knowingly" violates the act (or regulations under this act) shall be fined "not more than $1,000 or sentenced to prison for a term not to exceed one year, or both." However, any "subsequent violation of this act (or regulation) carries with it, potentially, a fine of "not more than $10,000" or a sentence of "not to exceed three years, or both." A special provision applies for farm labor contractors who violate section 106: the provision against the employment "with knowledge" of aliens. Hearings are permitted and the rights of the defendant are specified.

There is a private right of action. Any person "... may file suit in any district court of the United States having jurisdiction of the parties ... without regard to the citizenship of the parties and without regard to exhaustion of any alternative administrative remedies provided herein." Limitations on damages and equitable relief are spelled out.

No person shall be discriminated against for having, "with just cause, filed any complaint or instituted, or caused to be instituted, any proceeding under or related to this Act...." Appeal can be made to the Secretary of Labor. Any waiver of rights (except to the Secretary of Labor for enforcement purposes) "shall be void as contrary to public policy...."

Administrative Provisions. The Secretary of Labor "may issue such rules and regulations as are necessary to carry out this Act," consistent with the U.S. Code.

As may be appropriate, the Secretary may "investigate, and in connection wherewith, enter and inspect such places (including housing and vehicles) and such records (and make transcriptions thereof), question such persons and gather such information to determine compliance with this Act...." The Secretary "may issue subpoenas requiring the attendance and testimony of witnesses or the production of any evidence in connection with such investigations."

The Secretary may "enter into agreements with Federal and State agencies" in carrying out the program under MSPA.

Miscellaneous Provisions. "This Act is intended to supplement State law, and compliance with this Act shall not excuse any person from compliance with appropriate state law and regulation."

ADAMS FRUIT CO., INC. V. BARRETT

Perhaps only a consensus bill (such as that creating MSPA) could have been enacted under the circumstances. Yet, that would not end complaints, both pro and con. Migrant farmworkers, observed Representative Mickey Leland (D-TX) in 1985, just two years after MSPA was adopted, "are among the most vulnerable workers in our Nation." The conditions under which they live and work has resulted in "... an infant mortality rate that is two and one-half times the national average."[294] During the late 1980s, several Members protested about the alleged tendency of some Legal Services offices "to represent, or, I suggest, misrepresent, some of these migrant workers" in bringing complaints against farmers.[295] And, in 1993, Representative Miller argued that "Working and living conditions for migrant agricultural workers remain deplorable and in some cases have deteriorated" — and he introduced a comprehensive revision of MSPA.[296] The most serious complaint (one that would result in amendment of MSPA) grew out of the *Adams Fruit* case.[297]

A Ruling from the Court

In 1990, the U.S. Supreme Court ruled in *Adams Fruit Co.* v. *Barrett* that migrant farmworkers, employed by Adams Fruit Company, Inc., having "suffered severe injuries in an automobile accident" in an Adams Fruit van while traveling to work, had two options available for redress. They could file a claim under the Florida workmen's compensation law *and* they could avail themselves under the private right of action provision of MSPA.[298]

At issue before the Court was the question of exclusivity (or dual coverage) under the state and federal acts: i.e., worker's compensation *and* MSPA. The Court ruled that although Congress "may choose to establish state remedies as adequate alternatives to federal relief, it cannot be assumed that private federal rights of action are conditioned on the unavailability of state remedies absent some indication to that effect."[299]

In the view of the Court, no such alternative remedy was apparent. Adams Fruit argued that "in the absence of any explicit congressional statement regarding the preemptive scope" of MSPA, the Court should defer to the Department's position: i.e., a single remedy. The Court, however, rejected that view. It found that a "'gap' is not created in a statutory scheme merely because a statute does not restate the truism that States may not pre-empt federal law."[300] In summary, the Court held, "[o]ur review of the language and structure of AWPA [MSPA] leads us to conclude that AWPA does not establish workers' compensation benefits as an exclusive remedy...."[301]

Hearings on Workmen's Compensation

Representative Goodling branded the decision as "bad for employers" and "bad for workers" — allowing the worker "the ability to both recover workers' compensation *and* sue for compensatory and punitive damages." Goodling asserted: "As one who worked many long and hard hours in 1981 and 1982 to achieve the MSAWPA [MSPA] consensus[,] I intend to preserve it by pressing for early action next year ... to overturn the Adams Fruit decision."[302]

On September 15, 1993, Representative Austin Murphy (D-PA) called together at Fresno, California, a hearing by the Labor Standards Subcommittee. Two bills were on the table: H.R. 1173 (Miller) and H.R. 1999 by Victor Fazio (D-CA). The Miller bill was a comprehensive measure which, among other provisions, would have codified the *Adams Fruit* decision. The Fazio bill had for its sole purpose the overturning of that decision.[303] They had evolved, though from different perspectives, through "many months of unsuccessful negotiations aimed at producing consensus legislation to resolve the difficulties and concerns voiced by farmworker advocates and growers."[304]

As the Fresno hearings opened, several Members of Congress spoke. Richard Lehman (D-CA) and Calvin Dooley (D-CA) commenced with opposition to any new restrictions upon agricultural interests. They were followed by Howard Berman (D-CA) and by Miller, generally supportive of worker interests. The several Members emphasized the dichotomy existing over the prospective legislation. They were followed by representatives of organized labor, civil rights attorneys, and spokespersons for industry.[305]

On May 25, 1995, with a change in control in the House, Goodling became chair of the full Committee on Economic and Educational Opportunities. Cass Ballenger (R-NC) now chaired the Subcommittee on Workforce Protections with jurisdiction over agricultural labor. New hearings addressed the issues similarly. The Court, Ballenger stated, had interpreted MSPA "to provide for a private right of action for certain job related injuries, even if the individual was covered by workers' compensation at the time of the injury" leaving employers "exposed to potentially enormous liability for damages in spite of the fact that they have contributed into the workers' compensation system."[306] Conversely, Representative Major Owens (D-NY) suggested that "Instead of insuring work place protections, this committee is preoccupied with eliminating all inconveniences for the rich and privileged, at the expense of the working poor...."[307]

Bruce Wood, Senior Counsel for the American Insurance Association, argued that the Court's opinion was "not grounded on public policy" and that the Court had acted "narrowly and mechanically."[308] The "doctrine of exclusivity" was emphasized by Walter Kates, an industry representative. MSPA was "a consensus bill," he declared, with all parties in agreement that "the doctrine of workers' compensation exclusivity was a part" of the bill. The failure "to reverse the Adams Fruit decision," Kates stated, "could have adverse and unintentional consequences for both the farmer and the farmworker."[309] Steve Kenfield, a farm labor contractor from California, suggested that *Adams Fruit* "has complicated an already complex compliance situation." It "created frustration" in that payment of premiums for workers' compensation (mandatory in California) "is virtually meaningless." And, it suggested that "we could also face open-ended" liability. With others from industry, Kenfield called upon Congress to "reverse" the *Adams Fruit* decision.[310] Finally, David Moody, a former farmworker and the victim of an accident in Florida, testified about the problems and complexities of securing redress solely under the worker's compensation system.[311]

The Goodling Bill (1995)

On May 25, 1995, Representative Goodling introduced H.R. 1715, a bill dealing with workers' compensation benefits and MSPA. The bill was referred to the Committee on Economic and Educational Opportunities and passed.[312] Through the summer, discussions were conducted informally on the legislation and, in mid-October, Goodling was able to announce that a substitute would be offered for H.R. 1715 (with the same designation) that would carry with it the endorsement of Representatives Ballenger, Owens and William Clay (D-MO). [313]

The substitute version of H.R. 1715 provided that "where a State workers' compensation law is applicable and coverage is provided ... the workers' compensation benefits shall be the exclusive remedy for loss of such worker under this Act in the case of bodily injury or death...." In effect, *Adams Fruit* was overturned. The bill went on to discuss the expansion of statutory damages, the tolling of the statute of limitations under state workmen's compensation laws, disclosure of coverage (and processes) to the workers involved, and other matters. Mr. Goodling explained that H.R. 1715 "clarifies the relationship between workers compensation benefits and the private right of action" available under MSPA.[314]

Mr. Owens rose in support of the bill and expressed his appreciation to Representatives Goodling, Clay, and Ballenger — and to others: Representatives Miller, Berman and Fazio. "The efforts of all three gentlemen have been instrumental in the development of the amendment before us" — which he regarded as a "compromise."[315] Mr. Fazio argued that the bill "... is the result of 5 years of discussions, but it is a bill that needed to be enacted...."[316]

At this juncture, the House suspended the rules and passed the compromise version of H.R. 1715.[317] The bill was promptly dispatched to the Senate where, under unanimous consent, it was adopted.[318] On November 15, 1995, the measure was signed into law (P.L. 104-49) by President William Clinton.

Chapter 6

AGRICULTURAL WORKERS IN THE NEW CENTURY

For the most part, since the 1983 amendments (with the emergence of the Migrant and Seasonal Agricultural Workers Protection Act), the statute has remained largely unchanged, with the exception of the *Adams Fruit* legislation.[319]

The history of FLCRA (and, now, MSPA) has been long and tedious. For almost ten years (1964 to 1974), legislation remained in place but was, largely, unenforced — or, perhaps, unenforceable. Revised in 1974, there were serious attempts to enforce the statute but these seem to have required that many of the wrong people register (i.e., fixed site farmers, growers, and a variety of other agricultural interests) and, generally to comply with the act's restrictions. In 1983, FLCRA was repealed, and Congress started over with a new statute: the Migrant and Seasonal Agricultural Worker's Protection Act. The latter remains in place.

Debate over FLCRA and, to a lesser extent, MSPA, seems to have been exhausting. It could well be that some may now be disinclined to revisit the statute and to raise new questions. However, the need for oversight would seem to remain a priority where agricultural policy is concerned.

Thus far, in the 110th Congress, no new legislation to amend MSPA has been considered.

REFERENCES

[1]   Alexander Kendrick, *Prime Time: The Life of Edward R. Murrow* (Boston: Little, Brown and Company, 1969), p. 453.

[2]   U.S. Congress, Senate, Subcommittee on Migratory Labor of the Committee on Labor and Public Welfare. 86th Cong., 2nd Sess. (1960). Committee Print, *The Migrant Farm Worker in America*, p. 34. Report by Daniel H. Pollitt, et al. Cited hereafter as Pollitt, *The Migrant Farm Worker in America.*

[3]   Pollitt, *The Migrant Farm Worker in America*, pp. 36-38.

[4]   Ibid., pp. 34-36.

[5]   U.S. Congress, Senate Committee on Labor and Public Welfare, Subcommittee on Migratory Labor. *Migratory Labor.* Hearings, 87th Cong., 1st Sess., April 12-13, 1961, pp. 45-46. (Hereafter cited as Hearings, Senate, 1961.)   See also U.S. Congress, Senate, Subcommittee on Migratory Labor, Committee on Labor and Public Welfare. *Migratory Labor Bills.* 88th Cong., 1st Sess., April 10, 23, and 24, 1963, pp. 38-40. (Hereafter cited as Hearings, Senate, 1963.)

[6]   Hearings, Senate, 1961, p. 53.

[7]   James B. Moore, National Apple Institute, Hearings, Senate, 1961, p. 183.

[8]   Charles M. Creuziger, Vegetable Growers Association of America, Hearings, Senate, 1961, p. 82.

[9]   Carroll Miller, West Virginia State Horticultural Society, Hearings, Senate, 1961, p. 125.

[10] Hearings, Senate, 1961, p. 54. See U.S. Congress. House, Committee on Education and Labor, Subcommittee on Labor. *Migratory Labor.* Hearings, 87 Cong., 1st Sess., May 9-10, 1961, and May 19-20, 1961, p. 238 (Hereafter cited as Hearings, House, 1961.)

[11]   Hearings, House, 1963, p. 15.

[12]   Hearings, Senate, 1963, pp. 39-40. It would appear that the most frequent cause of concern, where farm labor contractors are involved, were problems associated in some manner with transportation. In the U.S. Congress, Senate, Committee on Labor and Public Welfare, 87th Cong., 1st Sess., Senate Report No. 695 to accompany S. 1162, August 9, 1961, p. 5, it is noted that "These abuses include overcharging workers for transportation advances, collecting for transportation expenses from both employers and workers, accepting transportation advances from employers and failing to report to work or reporting with a smaller crew than contracted for, abandoning a crew without means of transportation, and failure to return workers to their homes." (Cited hereafter as Senate Report No. 695, 1961.)

[13]   Hearings, Senate, 1963, p. 39. The reference was to a brochure, "Summary of Farm Labor Crew Leader Practices," November 1962, prepared by the Farm Labor Service, Bureau of Employment Security, Department of Labor.

[14]   Senate Report No. 695, 1961, p. 5. During Hearings, House, 1963, p. 97, there was a dialogue between Representative James Roosevelt and Edith E. Lowry, testifying on behalf of the National Advisory Committee on Farm Labor. "Mr. Roosevelt: ... We would also, for social security purposes, have a better way of seeing whether the proper deductions were being made and forwarded to the Federal Government rather than having, as we now suspect, but have very little way of proving, many of them pay social security to the crew leader and yet get no credit for it by the social security headquarters." "Would you consider this was too onerous a task for us to impose upon a crew leader?" "Miss Lowry: I don't think so because it seems to me it is essential for anybody who carries the responsibility of handling the affairs for so many people that find difficulty in fitting into our society to be required to handle these things in an orderly way." "I do know there is a real problem in the social security matter."

[15]   U.S. Congress, House, Committee on Labor, House Committee on Education and Labor, 88th Cong., 1st Sess., *Hearing, Registration of Farm Labor Contractors,* April 3, 5, and 10, 1963, p. 70. (Cited hereafter as Hearings, House, 1963.) Newman, p. 69, notes: "Because of their dependency on the crew leader, migrant workers are particularly vulnerable to exploitation and abuse by these contractors. Migrants," she explained, "are usually isolated from the community,

sometimes never even meeting the grower whose crop they pick. They are dependent on the crew leader for the next job, and for their daily living arrangements."

[16]   Hearings, Senate, 1963, p. 150. References to "this bill" or to "the bill" are generic. In some cases, it is not clear to which bill a speaker is referring or to an abstract bill. Further, reference is to a series of hearings with different bills.

[17]   Hearings, House, 1963, pp. 141-142.

[18]   Hearings, House, 1963, p. 22.

[19]   Hearings, House, 1963, p. 8.

[20]   Hearings, Senate, 1961, pp. 23-24.

[21]   Hearings, House, 1961, p. 116.

[22]   Hearings, House, 1963, p. 139.

[23]   Hearings, Senate, 1963, pp. 302-303.

[24]   Hearings, Senate, 1961, pp. 182-183.

[25]   Statement from the National Cotton Council, Hearings, House, 1961, p. 216.

[26]   Hearings, Senate, 1961, p. 63.

[27]   Hearings, House, 1963, p. 141.

[28]   Hearings, House, 1963, p. 10.

[29]   Hearings, House, 1961, p. 216.

[30]   Hearings, House, 1961, p. 206.

[31]   Hearings, Senate, 1961, p. 129.

[32]   Hearings, House, 1963, p. 143.

[33]   Hearings, House, 1961, p. 206.

[34]   Hearings, House, 1961, p. 176. (Italics added.)

[35]   Hearings, Senate, 1963, p. 161. On this issue, see Hearings, House, 1963, pp. 10-13, where there is a dialogue between Representative Roosevelt and Triggs of the Farm Bureau.

[36]   Hearings, House, 1963, p. 10.

[37]   Hearings, House, 1963, p. 120.

[38]   Hearings, Senate, 1963, p. 144.

[39]   Hearings, Senate, 1963, p. 227.

[40]   Hearings, Senate, 1963, pp. 227-228.

[41]   Hearings, House, 1963, p. 10.

[42]   Hearings, House, 1963, pp. 142-143.

[43]   Hearings, Senate, 1961, pp. 199-200.

[44]   Hearings, Senate, 1961, pp. 62-63.

[45]   Hearings, Senate, 1961, p. 174.

[46]   Hearings, House, 1961, p. 176. See also: Hearings, Senate 1961, pp. 62-63.

[47]   Hearings, House, 1961, pp. 32-33.

[48]   Hearings, House, 1961, p. 235. Mr. Fields went on to state that, in South Jersey, the prevailing wage was then $1.00.

[49]   The term *bracero* has a number of translations; but, in general, it refers to Mexican workers brought into the United States under a guest worker program. The bracero is a documented worker and should not be confused with the undocumented worker who has entered the United States illegally and, if employed, is employed illegally. See Howard N. Dillon, "Foreign Agricultural Workers and the Prevention of Adverse Effect," *Labor Law Journal,* December 1966, pp. 739-748; and CRS Report RL32044, *Immigration: Policy Considerations Related to Guest Worker Programs,* by Andorra Bruno.

[50]   8 U.S.C. 1188(a)(A) and (B). See also CRS Report RL32861, *Farm Labor: The Adverse Effect Wage Rate (AEWR),* by William G. Whittaker.

[51]   Hearings, House, 1961, p. 211.

[52]   Hearings, House, 1961, p. 4.

[53]   Hearings, Senate, 1963, pp. 125-126.

[54]   Hearings, House, 1961, p. 145.

[55]   Hearings, House, 1961, p. 101.

[56]   Hearings, House, 1961, p. 103.

[57]   Hearings, House, 1963, pp. 136-137. Father Vizzard urged against the use of immigrant workers. On page 149, he suggested "... I don't think the way to help the Mexican economy or the individual Mexican people is by using them as, in effect, strikebreakers against our own people, for undercutting the wages and working conditions of our own citizens." See also comments of Senator Williams, Hearings, House, 1961, p. 53.

[58]   Hearings, House, 1963, p. 124.

[59]   Hearings, House, 1963, pp. 50-51.

[60]   Hearings, House, 1963, p. 51. Reference was to prior comments that sugar companies would not need to be covered since they were not involved (or only marginally involved) in recruitment, and they are fixed site employers.

[61]   Hearings, House, 1963, pp. 51-53.

[62]   *Congressional Record,* June 11, 1963, pp. 10619-10621.

[63]   *Congressional Record,* June 11, 1963, p. 10621.

[64]   *Congressional Record*, June 11, 1963, p. 10625.

[65]   *Congressional Record*, August 17, 1964, pp. 19894-19895.

[66]   *Congressional Record*, August 17, 1964, p. 19895.

[67]   *Congressional Record*, August 17, 1964, pp. 19895-19896.

[68]   *Congressional Record*, August 17, 1964, p. 19896.

[69]   *Congressional Record*, August 21, 1964, pp. 20874-20877.

[70]   All quotations, here, are from P.L. 88-582. However, the reader is urged to consult the statute for more specific details.

[71]   See *Federal Register*, December 22, 1964, p. 18157, and February 3, 1965, p. 1139. It was not until late 1972 that responsibility for FLCRA was shifted to the Wage/Hour Division which normally deals with labor standards issues. See *Federal Register*, January 17, 1973, p. 1636.

[72]   See *Federal Register*, October 12, 1966, pp. 13174-13176, November 22, 1966, pp. 14772-14775, May 9, 1967, pp. 7025-7026, and July 20, 1967, p. l0649.

[73]   *Federal Register*, March 6, 1965, pp. 2945-2950. For example, the rule states, "... if a person intends to recruit five (5) migrant workers one day for Farmer A and the next day is requested to recruit and does recruit eight (8) migrant workers for Farmer B, these are separate and independent acts and do not total up to thirteen (13) for purposes of the statutory requirement. However, if he has contracts to hire a total of eighteen (18) migrant workers for Farmers X, Y, and Z and he hires this number as a result of three days effort, the statutory amount of 'ten or more' would be present." But it concludes, "... the application of these principles to other situations will depend on all the facts."

[74]   *Federal Register*, April 15, 1969, pp. 6502-6504.

[75]   *Federal Register*, October 20, 1972, p. 22660.

[76]   See *Federal Register*, January 17, 1973, pp. 1636-1637, and August 24, 1973, p. 22778.

[77]   Father John Kelly, Our Lady of Lourdes Church, Seaford, Delaware, stated that there had been "a tremendous overlapping of intermeshing authorities...." He continued: "... we have federal regulations, we have state regulations and we have local county implementation." Kelly further observed, "When one has a problem you have to deal with the hour and wage [laws] and to deal with social security, you have to deal with health, education and welfare, you have to deal with the local labor office and no one in any of these departments is quite clear where" the migrant worker is located with respect to the several

jurisdictions. "You can spend days trying to establish a relationship with any particular office and no one is sure at the end of the day whether he has a reason or not to handle your problem. Now for an illiterate perhaps non-English speaking person, the difficulty is multiplied 1,000 times. And the man who is supposed to solve all these problems is the crew leader." Representative William Ford (D-MI) would later concede, "We are painfully aware that it is very difficult to tie it all together because of the multitude of Federal agencies that have fragmented responsibilities in this area." See U.S. Congress, House, Subcommittee on Agricultural Labor, Committee on Education and Labor, *Farm Labor Contractor Registration Act Amendments of 1973*, pp. 179 and 183. (Cited hereafter as Hearings, House, 1973.)

[78]   U.S. Congress, Senate, Subcommittee on Employment, Poverty, and Migratory Labor, Committee on Labor and Public Welfare. *Farm Labor Contractor Registration Act Amendments, 1974.* Fresno, Cal., February 8, 1974, and Washington, D.C., April 9, 1974, p. 2. (Cited hereafter as Hearings, Senate, 1974.)

[79]   Hearings, Senate, 1974, p. 107.

[80]   Hearings, Senate, 1974, pp. 152-153. The speaker was Father James Vizzard, then of the United Farm Workers.

[81]   Hearings, Senate, 1974, pp. 115-116.

[82]   Hearings, House, 1973, pp. 108-109.

[83]   Hearings, House, 1973, p. 107.

[84]   Hearings, House, 1973, pp. 107-108.

[85]   Hearings, House, 1973, p. 60.

[86]   Hearings, Senate, 1974, pp. 230-231.

[87]   Hearings, Senate, 1974, pp. 217-218.

[88]   Hearings, Senate, 1974, p. 36.

[89]   Hearings, Senate, 1974, p. 110.

[90]   Hearings, House, 1974, p. 109.

[91]   Hearings, House, 1973, p. 55.

[92]   Hearings, Senate, 1974, p. 50. See also Hearings, Senate, 1974, p. 110, and Hearings, House, 1973, p. 108.

[93]   Hearings, House, 1973, p. 108.

[94]   Hearings, Senate, 1974, pp. 49-50.

[95]   Hearings, Senate, 1974, p. 105.

[96]   Hearings, Senate, 1974, p. 43.

[97]   Hearings, Senate, 1974, p. 45.

[98]   Hearings, Senate, 1974, p. 41.

[99]   Hearings, Senate, 1974, p. 105.

[100]   Hearings, House, 1973, p. 165. The speaker, Joe Alexander, is a former farm labor contractor from Homestead, Florida.

[101]   Hearings, House, 1973, p. 63.

[102]   Hearings, House, 1973, p. 155. See also Hearings, House, p. 118. DOL did have grower complaints concerning funds forwarded to cover transportation costs of farmworkers.

[103]   Hearings, Senate, 1974, pp. 154-156.

[104]   Hearings, Senate, 1974, pp. 323-324.

[105]   Hearings, House, 1973, p. 64.

[106]   Hearings, House, 1973, p. 92.

[107]   Hearings, Senate, 1974, p. 32-33.

[108]   Hearings, Senate, 1974, p. 163.

[109]   Hearings, Senate, 1974, p. 142.

[110]   Hearings, Senate, 1974, p. 172.

[111]   Hearings, Senate, 1974, p. 35.

[112]   Hearings, Senate, 1974, p. 35. See also Hearings, Senate, 1974, p. 154, for an analysis by C. H. Fields of the Farm Bureau.

[113]   Hearings, House, 1973, p. 174.

[114]   Hearings, House, 1973, p. 63.

[115]   Hearings, House, 1973, p. 94. Sweeney proposed inclusion of day haulers in the bill.

[116]   Hearings, House, 1973, p. 174.

[117]   Hearings, House, 1973, p. 97. DeLury also stated: "In addition, some day-haul work is interstate; this activity is covered under the current act. We oppose a change which would exempt this interstate activity." See also DeLury, Hearings, Senate, 1974, pp. 117, 147-148.

[118]   Hearings, House, 1973, p. 23.

[119]   Hearings, House, 1973, p. 102.

[120]   Hearings, House, 1973, p. 86.

[121]   Hearings, House, 1973, p. 23.

[122]   Hearings, House, 1973, p. 63. David Sweeney and William Grami, both from the Teamsters, noted their support of intrastate coverage. See Hearings, House, 1973, p. 187.

[123]   Hearings, House, 1973, p. 97.

[124]   Hearings, Senate, 1974, p. 220. Under the 1964 legislation, growers who recruited "solely for his own operation," were not covered.

[125]   Hearings, Senate, 1974, p. 156.

[126]   Hearings, House, 1973, pp. 190-191.

[127]   See Section 3(b)(2) of P.L. 88-582.

[128] Hearings, Senate, 1974, p. 49.

[129] Hearings, Senate, 1974, p. 249.

[130] Hearings, Senate, 1974, p. 37.

[131] Hearings, Senate, 1974, p. 116. (Italics added.)

[132] Hearings, House, 1973, p. 104.

[133] Hearings, Senate, 1974, pp. 49-50.

[134] Hearings, House, 1973, pp. 87-88. See also Hearings, Senate, 1961, p. 130.

[135] Hearings, Senate, 1974, pp. 226-227.

[136] Hearings, Senate, 1974, pp. 183-184. See also, ibid, pp. 170-172.

[137] Hearings, Senate, 1974, pp. 245-246. (Italics added.)

[138] Hearings, Senate, 1974, p. 260. Phelan added: "Moreover, this provision poses the question of whether you are crossing jurisdictional lines with the Committee on the Judiciary. You will recall that this language was included in the proposed amendment to the Fair Labor Standards Act last year and was subsequently dropped for that reason."

[139] Hearings, Senate, 1974, p. 163.

[140] Hearings, House, 1973, pp. 89-90.

[141] *Congressional Record*, March 7, 1974, p. 5694. Original sponsors were: Earl Landgrebe (R-IN), Ella Grasso (D-CN), Frank Thompson (D-NJ), Gus Hawkins (D-CA), William Lehman (D-FL), James O'Hara (D-MI), Lloyd Meeds (D-WA), Albert Quie (R-MN), David Towell (R-NV), William Steiger (R-WI), John Erlenborn (R-IL), and Orval Hansen (R-ID).

[142] *Congressional Record*, May 7, 1974, pp. 13402-13405.

[143] *Congressional Record*, May 7, 1974, p. 13405.

[144] *Congressional Record*, May 7, 1974, p. 13406.

[145] *Congressional Record*, May 7, 1974, p. 13406.

[146] *Congressional Record*, May 7, 1974, pp. 13408-13409.

[147] *Congressional Record*, May 7, 1974, p. 13409.

[148] *Congressional Record*, May 8, 1974, p. 13619.

[149] *Congressional Record*, October 3, 1974, pp. 33745-33746.

[150] *Congressional Record*, October 3, 1974, p. 33746.

[151] *Congressional Record*, October 3, 1974, p. 33746.

[152] *Congressional Record*, October 3, 1974, p. 33747.

[153] *Congressional Record*, October 11, 1974, pp. 35468-35471.

[154] *Congressional Record*, October 11, 1974, p. 35471.

[155] *Congressional Record,* October 16, 1974, pp. 35901-35902. Both Senators Hatfield and Magnuson specifically endorsed the day haul provisions of the bill. However, for the next several Congresses, that provision (in the context of youth labor under the Fair Labor Standards Act) would remain very controversial.

[156] *Congressional Record,* October 16, 1974, p. 35902.

[157] *Congressional Record,* October 16, 1974, p. 35903.

[158] *Congressional Record,* November 18, 1974, pp. 36246-36247.

[159] *Congressional Record,* March 20, 1974, p. 7383.

[160] *Congressional Record,* November 21, 1974, p. 36822.

[161] *Congressional Record,* November 22, 1974, pp. 37040-37042.

[162] *Congressional Record,* November 26, 1974, pp. 37372-37376.

[163] *Congressional Record,* December 11, 1974, p. 39005.

[164] See P.L. 93-518 for precise wording of the amendments.

[165] U.S. Congress, House, Committee on Education and Labor, Subcommittee on Agricultural Labor, *Oversight Hearings on the Farm Labor Contractor Registration Act,* Hearings, 94th Cong., 1st Sess., October 1 and October 11, 1975, pp. 113-136. (Hereafter cited as Hearings, House, 1975.)

[166] Hearings, House, 1975, p. 10.

[167] Hearings, House, 1975, pp. 10-11. On Congressional opinion, see pp.85 and 93-94.

[168] Hearings, House, 1975, p. 15.

[169] Hearings, House, 1975, p. 16. DOL's failure to publish regulations for the 1974 amendments seemed to permeate the entire proceedings. Robert Mills, Salinas Valley Independent Growers' Association (p. 284), stated: "I think the whole effort of the testimony here today is, please, may we have some definitive regulations from the Department of Labor and not try to define what we believe the intent of Congress is...." Similarly, Donald Dressler, Western Growers' Association (p. 273), taking note of litigation then before the courts, stated, "We would wish ... that the court would have required the Department to first draft regulations before they ran off in all these different directions."

[170] Hearings, House, 1975, p. 13. As of Sept 20, 1975, DeLury testified, "we had issued 3,718 certificates" — more than in prior years but less than expected with "approximately 10,000 or more" contractors that should be subject to coverage under the act.

[171] Hearings, House, 1975, p. 14.

[172] Hearings, House, 1975, p. 106.

[173] Hearings, House, 1975, p. 53.

[174] Hearings, House, 1975, p. 15.

[175] Hearings, House, 1975, p. 16. Regulations were proposed, December 8, 1975, *Federal Register*, pp. 57332-5733.

[176] Hearings, House, 1975, pp. 258-259.

[177] Hearings, House, 1975, p. 270.

[178] Hearings, House, 1975, p. 252.

[179] Hearings, House, 1975, p. 14. DeLury continued: "Certainly an employee of a grower, whether full-time or not, who devotes all of his time or the majority of his time *to farm labor contractor activities* is not within the exemption and such an employee should register under the law." (Italics added.)

[180] Hearings, House, 1975, p. 261.

[181] Hearings, House, 1975, p. 280.

[182] Hearings, House, 1975, p. 68.

[183] Hearings, House, 1975, p. 280.

[184] Hearings, House, 1975, p. 14.

[185] Hearings, House, 1975, pp. 16-18.

[186] Hearings, House, 1975, p. 97.

[187] Hearings, House, 1975, pp. 258-259.

[188] Hearings, House, 1975, p. 100.

[189] Hearings, House, 1975, pp. 19-20.

[190] Comments of Perry Ellsworth for management, Hearings, House, 1975, pp. 89-93.

[191] Hearings, House, 1975, p. 82.

[192] Hearings, House, 1975, p. 94.

[193] Hearings, House, 1975, p. 270.

[194] Gordon testified, Hearings, House, 1975, p. 285: "They operate dining facilities, and in some cases provide hot meals in the orchards. These camps provide recreation facilities, television rooms, chapels, and in some cases they provide counseling for the workers. This housing and attendant facilities are provided on a cost or below cost basis to the workers."

[195] Hearings, House, 1975, pp. 285-287.

[196] See Section 5(a)(2) of the act. The Secretary had some measure of discretion in this matter.

[197] Statement of Scott Toothaker, Texas Citrus & Vegetable Growers & Shippers, Hearings, House 1975, pp. 67-69. Italics added.

[198] Hearings, House, 1975, p. 20. See also section on *Adams Fruit* litigation, below.

[199] Hearings, House, 1975, p. 52.

[200] Hearings, House, 1975, pp. 52-54.

[201] Hearings, House, 1975, p. 54. This conversation took place some twenty years after the end of the bracero program.

[202] Hearings, House, 1975, p. 106.

[203] Hearings, House, 1975, pp. 106-107.

[204] Hearings, House, 1975, p. 107. Nomellini questioned, p. 98, the ability of the "foreman and supervisors who are not sophisticated interrogators" to screen for illegal immigration. "If it is your desire to keep illegal aliens out of the country then cooperation from the State Department will be required and still penalties will have to be imposed upon the apprehended illegal alien himself." He added: "The slap on the hand and free transportation to Mexico is not an adequate deterrent." See also pp. 146-148.

[205] Hearings, House, 1975, p. 77.

[206] Hearings, House, 1975, p. 262.

[207] Hearings, House, 1957, pp. 277-279.

[208] *Federal Register*, June 1976, p. 26820. See also *Federal Register*, December 8, 1975, pp. 57332-57339, for the proposed regulations.

[209] *Federal Register*, June 29, 1976, p. 26820.

[210] *Federal Register,* June 29, 1976, pp. 26825-26826.

[211] *Congressional Record*, March 4, 1976, p. 5571.

[212] *Congressional Record,* March 9, 1976, pp. 5955, 5956-5957, and March 11, 1976, p. 6192.

[213] *Congressional Record*, March 17, 1976, pp. 6802-6803.

[214] *Congressional Record,* March 18, 1976, p. 7108. See letter of Representative Ford and Senator Nelson to William Usery, Secretary of Labor, February 23, 2976, reprinted in *Congressional Record,* March 23, 1976, p. 7611.

[215] *Congressional Record,* March 18, 1976, pp. 7108-7110.

[216] *Congressional Record*, March 23, 1976, pp. 7719 and 7720.

[217] *Congressional Record*, March 23, 1976, p. 7689.

[218] Ibid. Representative Bedell explained: "The original act exempted crews employing less than 10 people from its registration requirements. However, in 1974, the statute was amended to include any group which 'recruits or transports' more than one employee. This numerical change technically brought small custom combiners and sheep shearers under the law despite the fact that there is no specific reference to these groups in the legislative history of the act."

[219] *Congressional Record*, March 23, 1976, pp. 7608-7612.

[220] *Congressional Record*, March 24, 1976, pp. 7785-7786.

[221] *Congressional Record*, March 24, 1976, p. 7786.

[222] *Congressional Record*, April 6, 1976, p. 9554.

[223] *Congressional Record*, July 26, 1976, pp. 23735-23741. See H.R. 10133 (94th Congress).

[224] *Congressional Record,* September 30, 1976, pp. 33815-33816, 33866-33867.

[225] *Congressional Record*, October 1, 1976, pp. 35170-35171.

[226] U.S. Congress, House, Committee on Education and Labor, Subcommittee on Economic Opportunity. *Farm Labor Contractor Registration Act,* Hearings, 95th Cong., 2nd Sess., February 22-23, 1978, pp. 35-36. (Cited hereafter as Hearings, House, 1978.)

[227] Hearings, House, 1978, pp. 36-37. Rep. Charles Grassley (R-IA), p. 49, questioned the "loss of an important source of youth employment." Rep. Charles Thone (R-NE), p. 43, argued that "such stupid regulations" might force companies to turn "to mechanical methods of detasseling and then what would this do to our employment problems?" In a letter, February 28, 1978, pp. 40-41, later submitted for the record, Smith wrote to Secretary Marshall and explained: "We have thousands and thousands of workers who will be affected by this matter and are waiting to see if their government has the capacity to exercise some restraint in its authority, and some common sense in its actions." See testimony of Representative David Stockman (R-MI), ibid, pp. 45-48, and comments of Richard O'Connell, National Council of Farmer Cooperatives, Hearings, Senate, April 1963, pp. 199-200.

[228] *Congressional Record,* April 11, 1978, p. 9697.

[229] *Congressional Record*, April 25, 1978, p. 11363.

[230] *Congressional Record*, September 8, 1978, pp. 28565-28566. Senator Richard Lugar (R-IN) stated, p. 28568: "Activities exempted include detasseling but also include activities such as roguing and hand pollenation which are typically performed by young people."

[231] Congressional Record, September 8, 1978, p. 28566.

[232] See comments of Senator Williams (D-NJ), September 8, 1978, *Congressional Record*, pp. 28568-28569, about the seed corn industry.

[233] *Congressional Record*, September 8, 1978, p. 28566.

[234] *Congressional Record,* September 8, 1978, p. 28568.

[235] *Congressional Record*, October 13, 1978, pp. 36707-36709, 37113-37114.

[236] *Congressional Record*, June 25, 1978, p. 16748.

[237] See John McFall to Ray Marshall, June 30, 1977, reprinted in U.S. Congress, House, Committee on Education and Labor, Subcommittee on Economic Opportunity, *Farm Labor Contractor Act,* Hearings, 95th Cong., 2nd Sess., February 22-23, 1978, pp. 13-14. (Cited hereafter as Hearings, House, 1978.) Others joining McFall in his inquiry to Marshall were Robert Leggett, John Moss, B. F. Sisk, and Harold Johnson, all Democrats from California.

[238] Hearings, House, 1978, pp. 14-16.

[239] Hearings, House, 1978, p. 78.

[240] Hearings, House, 1978, pp. 13, 42-43, and 48.

[241] Hearings, House, 1978, pp. 21-28. Current radius was 25 miles.

[242] Hearings, House, 1978, p. 23.

[243] Hearings, House, 1978, p. 8. The correspondence between Rep. Sisk and Elisburg appears on pages 7-12. See also comments by Rep. McFall on this issue, pp. 18-19.

[244] Hearings, House, 1978, pp. 45-47. When introducing FLCRA legislation, Stockman referred to "predatory bureaucrats" that have turned the law into "a weapon against the farmer." He explained (*Congressional Record,* June 20, 1977, p. 19982): "In the Department of Labor's eyes, the expectation that the laborers would return to his farm became 'valuable consideration' to the farmer entering into a casual agreement with his neighbor. This play upon words turned the farmers, he said, into 'farm labor contractors.'"

[245] Hearings, House, 1978, p. 52.

[246] Hearings, House, 1978, p. 52.

[247] Hearings, House, 1978, pp. 54-55.

[248] *Congressional Record*, June 20, 1977, p. 19982.

[249] *Congressional Record,* May 21, 1979, p. 11996. The Panetta proposal was only one of a number of FLCRA-related bills that surfaced during the late 1970s and early 1980s.

[250] See J. Bennett Johnston, with 51 other Members of the Senate, to F. Ray Marshall, October 24, 1979, reprinted in the *Congressional Record,* November 14, 1979, pp. 32322-32323.

[251] Labor Secretary Marshall to J. Bennett Johnston (with others), *Congressional Record*, December 18, 1979, pp. 36850-36851.

[252] Senators J. Bennett Johnston and Russell B. Long to Labor Secretary Marshall , reprinted in *Congressional Record*, July 24, 1980, p. 19561.

[253] *Congressional Record*, July 24, 1980, p. 19557.

[254] *Congressional Record*, July 24, 1980, pp. 19557-19558. Among groups backing his amendment, Senator Boren listed: "The American Soybean Association; the American Farm Bureau Federation, with some 3 million farmers as members; the American Frozen Food Institute; the American Mushroom Institute; the American Seed Trade Association; the American Sod Producers Association; the American Sugar Beet Growers Association; the Florida Citrus Processors Association; the Florida Sugar Cane League; the International Apple Institute; the National Broiler Council; the National Institute of Wheat Growers; the National Cattleman's Association; the National Cotton Council; the National Council of Agricultural Employers; the National Council of Farmer Cooperatives; the National Food Processors Association; the National Grange, with more than 500,000 members, made up of farmers; the National Meat Association; the National Peach Council; the Pennsylvania Food Processors Association; the Rio Grande Valley Sugar Growers Cooperative; the Society of American Florists; the United Fresh Fruit and Vegetable Association; and the Western Growers Association."

[255] *Congressional Record*, July 24, 1980, pp. 19558-19564.
[256] *Congressional Record*, July 24, 1980, p. 19574.
[257] *Congressional Record*, December 18, 1979, p. 36851.
[258] *Congressional Record,* July 24, 1980, p. 19456.
[259] *Congressional Record,* July 24, 1980, p. 19457.
[260] *Congressional Record*, August 26, 1980, pp. 23411-23413.
[261] *Congressional Record*, September 9, 1980, pp. 28405-28406.
[262] *Congressional Record*, September 9, 1980, pp. 24805-24807.
[263] *Congressional Record*, September 10, 1980, pp. 25102-25103.
[264] *Congressional Quarterly Almanac* (1980), Washington: Congressional Quarterly Inc., 1981, p. 453.
[265] *Congressional Record*, April 8, 1981, p. 6941. As a result of the 1980 election, Ray Marshall was replaced as Labor Secretary by Raymond J. Donovan.
[266] *Congressional Record*, April 8, 1981, p. 6943.
[267] In the 96th Congress, the Panetta bill carried the names of 160 Members. See *Congressional Record,* May 20, 1981, p. 10353.
[268] *Congressional Record*, May 20, 1991, p. 10353.
[269] *Congressional Record*, May 20, 1981, pp. 10353-10354.
[270] *Congressional Record,* May 20, 2981, p. 10354. Both the Boren and Panetta bills were superceded by the Administration's bill, introduced by request by Representative Miller.

[271] U.S. Congress. House. Subcommittee on Labor Standards, Committee on Education and Labor, *Hearings on the Migrant and Seasonal Agricultural Worker Protection Act,* September 14, 1982, p. 1. (Cited hereafter as Hearings, House, 1982.)

[272] U.S. Congress, House, Committee on Education and Labor, *Migrant and Seasonal Agricultural Worker Protection Act,* H.Rept. 97-885, September 28, 1982, p. 4. (Cited hereafter as House, Committee Report 97-885, September 28, 1982.)

[273] Hearings, House, 1982, p. 43.

[274] Hearings, House, 1982, p. 44. Collyer, p.50, proceeded to thank "all those persons and organizations who participated in the cooperative effort over the past 18 months to develop this legislation."

[275] See testimony of Jay Power, Legislative Representative, AFL-CIO, and of Perry Ellsworth, National Council of Agricultural Employers, Hearings, House, 1982, pp. 54-60.

[276] See testimony of William Beardall, staff attorney, Texas Rural Legal Aid, Marc Schacht of the Farmworker Justice Fund, and Garry B. Bryant, an attorney from Tucson with several years representing agricultural employees, Hearings, House, 1982, pp. 60-173.

[277] Hearings, House, 1982, p. 174. See also Representative Panetta's statement, September 14, 1982, p. 23441. Panetta was a co-sponsor of the legislation.

[278] House, Committee Report 97-885, September 28, 1982, p. 1.

[279] House, Committee Report 97-885, September 28, 1982, p. 3.

[280] *Congressional Record,* September 28, 1982, p. 25609.

[281] *Congressional Record,* September 29, 1982, p. 25609.

[282] *Congressional Record,* September 29, 1982, pp. 26008-26010.

[283] *Congressional Record,* September 29, 1982, p. 25866.

[284] *Congressional Record,* December 19, 1982, pp. 32458-32466.

[285] Public Papers of the President of the United States. *Ronald Reagan, 1983. Book 1, January 1 to July 1, 1983.* Washington, U.S. Government Printing Office, 1984, p. 47.

[286] See the *Adams Fruit* case, discussed below.

[287] All language, where in quotation marks, in this section is taken from P.L. 97-470. However, some variation may result from codification and from subsequent amendments that impinge upon the act. This is a summary. The reader may want to consult the current text of MSPA.

[288] This section was subsequently repealed and its substance was moved to Title VIII, Aliens and Nationality, as part of the general restructuring under the Immigration Reform and Control Act of 1986.

[289] In the section on definitions, discussed above, it is stated: "(8)(A) Except as provided in subparagraph (B), the term 'migrant agricultural worker' means an individual who is employed in agricultural employment of a seasonal or other temporary nature, and who is required to be absent overnight from his permanent place of residence. (B) The term "migrant agricultural worker" does not include — (i) any immediate family member of an agricultural employer or a farm labor contractor; or (ii) any temporary nonimmigrant alien who is authorized to work in agricultural employment in the United States under sections 101(a)(15)(H)(ii) and 214(c) of the Immigration and Nationality Act."

[290] DOL will make available the necessary linguistic forms.

[291] In the section on definitions, it is stated, "(10)(A) Except as provided in subparagraph (B), the term 'seasonal agricultural worker' means an individual who is employed in agricultural employment of a seasonal or other temporary nature and is not required to be absent overnight from his permanent place of residence — (i) when employed on a farm or ranch performing field work related to planting, cultivating, or harvesting operations; or (ii) when employed in canning, packing, ginning, seed conditioning or related research, or processing operations, and transported, or caused to be transported, to or from the place of employment by means of a day-haul operation. (B) The term 'seasonal agricultural worker' does not include — (i) any migrant agricultural worker; (ii) any immediate family member of an agricultural employer or a farm labor contractor; or (iii) any temporary nonimmigrant alien who is authorized to work in agricultural employment in the United States under sections 101(a)(15)(H)(ii) and 214(c) of the Immigration and National Act."

[292] DOL will make available the necessary linguistic forms.

[293] See discussion, below, under *Adams Fruit.*

[294] *Congressional Record*, September 1985, p. 22927.

[295] *Congressional Record*, September 30, 1986, pp. 27399-27401, March 6, 1987, pp. 5048-5049, and July 17, 1989, p. 14919.

[296] *Congressional Record*, March 2, 1993, pp. 3953 and 3937. See also H.R. 1173 of the 103rd Congress.

[297] *Congressional Record,* October 27, 1990, p. 37188.

[298] 494 U.S. 638, 640 (1989).

[299] 494 U.S. 638, 639 (1989).

[300] 494 U.S. 638, 649 (1989).

[301] 494 U.S. 638, 650 (1989).

[302] *Congressional Record,* October 27, 1990, p. 37188. At the close of
       the 102nd Congress, an amendment was added to the Legislative
       Branch Appropriations Act (H.R. 5427), suspending for a brief period
       the impact of the *Adams Fruit* decision. See *Congressional Record,*
       October 3, 1992, p. 31243, and October 5, 1992, p. 31598.
[303] See also S. 1450 (Feinstein) to overturn *Adams Fruit.* None of the
       bills was enacted.
[304] U.S. Congress, House, Subcommittee on Labor Standards,
       Occupational Health and Safety, Committee on Education and Labor,
       Hearing on H.R. 1173 and H.R. 1999. September 15, 1993, p. 1.
       (Cited hereafter as Hearings, House, 1993.) See also for general
       reaction to the MSPA, U.S. Congress, Subcommittee on Labor
       Standards, Committee on Education and Labor, *Oversight Hearings
       on the Migrant and Seasonal Agricultural Worker Protection Act,*
       July 13, 1987. The 1987 hearing was conducted in Biglerville, Pa.
[305] Hearings, House, 1993, p. 48.
[306] U.S. Congress, House, Subcommittee on Workforce Protections,
       Committee on Economic and Educational Opportunities,. *Hearings on
       Adams Fruit Co., Inc. V. Barrett.* May 25, 1995, pp. 1-2. (Cited
       hereafter as Hearings, House, 1995.)
[307] Hearings, House, 1995, p. 2.
[308] Hearings, House, 1995, p. 5.
[309] Hearings, House, 1995, pp. 12-14. Kates is identified as representing
       the National Council of Agricultural Employers (as chairman of their
       Migrant and Seasonal Agricultural Worker Protection Act
       Committee), the Florida Fruit and Vegetable Association (as director
       of their Labor Relations Division), and the Workers' Compensatory
       Integrity, Stability, and Equity Coalition.
[310] Hearings, House, 1995, pp. 16-19.
[311] Hearings, House, 1995, pp. 21-22.
[312] *Congressional Record,* May 25, 1995, pp. 14444 and 14641.
[313] *Congressional Record,* October 13, 1995, pp. 28027-28028. On
       October 17, 1995, p. 28126, Mr. Goodling explained that the original
       bill had been reported from the Committee on Economic and
       Educational Opportunities but, after several weeks of negotiations, he
       was now able to offer a consensus bill.
[314] *Congressional Record,* October 17, 1995, pp. 28125-28127.
[315] *Congressional Record,* October 17, 1995, p. 28127.
[316] *Congressional Record,* October 17, 1995, p. 28128.
[317] *Congressional Record,* October 17, 1995, p. 28129.

[318] *Congressional Record,* October 31, 1995, p. 30907.

[319] See U.S. Congress. House. Subcommittee on Workforce Protections, Committee on Education and the Workforce. *Field Hearing on Issues Relating to Migrant and Seasonal Agricultural Workers and Their Employers* (Newland, N.C.), 105th Cong., 1st Sess., September 12, 1997, 164 pp.; and U.S. Congress. House. Subcommittee on Workforce Protections, Committee on Education and the Workforce. 105th Cong., 2nd Sess., *The Effect of the Fair Labor Standards Act on Amish Families and H.R. 2028, The MSPA Clarification Act.* April 21, 1998, 167 pp.

INDEX

A

access, 14
Adams, 67, 68, 69, 70, 71, 82, 87, 88, 89
Adams Fruit, 2, 67, 69
administration, 12, 20, 40, 44, 51, 57, 58, 59
administrative, 8, 12, 20, 66
age, 11, 28, 45, 52
agent (s), 2, 37, 43, 47, 55
agricultural, vii, viii, 1, 2, 5, 7, 14, 15, 19, 20, 25, 26, 31, 37, 39, 40, 42, 43, 44, 49, 53, 54, 55, 56, 57, 58, 59, 60, 61, 62, 63, 64, 65, 66, 67, 69, 71, 87, 88
agricultural association, 63, 64, 65
agricultural employer, 63, 64, 65, 88
agriculture, vii, 11, 15, 16, 26, 31, 38, 43, 57
aid, 17
alcoholic beverages, 4
alien (s), 11, 27, 31, 32, 34, 38, 35, 46, 47, 48, 64, 66, 83, 88
alternative (s), 66, 68
amendments, 2, 28, 30, 33, 36, 38, 39, 40, 43, 49, 50, 51, 53, 56, 58, 59, 61, 71, 81, 87
American Farm Bureau Federation, 5, 61, 86

anger, 55
application, 16, 41, 77
appropriations, 20, 23, 25
Arizona, 44
assessment, 20
assets, 55
associations, 8, 42, 63
attention, vii, 33, 41
Attorney General, 34, 38, 46, 64
attorneys, 69
authority, 7, 9, 13, 20, 23, 50, 58, 84
availability, 6
awareness, 31

B

B. F. Sisk, 54, 85
beating, 4
benefits, 40, 68, 70
benevolence, 7
beverages, 4
birth, 49
blame, 52
bodily injury, 70
bonding, 10
bookkeeping, 5
Border Patrol, 32, 46, 47
Boston, 73
breeding, 51, 64
bureaucracy, 45, 58

buses, 27, 45
business, 7, 8, 13, 25, 29, 32, 55, 56

C

California, 26, 27, 39, 41, 42, 44, 46, 60,
    68, 69, 85
capacity, 8, 29, 84
carrier, 64
Catholic, 11
certainty, 61
certificate, 8, 9, 15, 16, 20, 21, 31, 33,
    37, 46, 49, 64, 66
certification, 8, 16
charitable, 7, 15, 54, 63
child labor, 4
children, 45
citizens, 34, 48, 76
citizenship, 66
civil rights, 69
clients, 41, 61
Colorado, 23
commission, 4, 64, 65
Committee on the Judiciary, 80
commodity (ies), 32, 37, 44, 65
common carriers, 45
community, 55, 74
compensation, 31, 54, 68, 69, 70
competence, 24
compliance, 22, 40, 67, 69
conditioning, 88
conflict, 23
Congress, vii, viii, 1, 2, 6, 10, 14, 20, 25,
    30, 33, 36, 39, 40, 43, 47, 49, 50, 53,
    56, 57, 59, 60, 68, 69, 71, 73, 74, 78,
    81, 84, 85, 86, 87, 88, 89, 90
Congressional Record, 76, 77, 80, 81,
    83, 84, 85, 86, 87, 88, 89, 90
consensus, 61, 67, 68, 69, 89
consent, 70
Constitution, 46
constitutional, 46
constraints, 46
continuing, 59

contractors, 2, 3, 5, 6, 8, 10, 13, 14, 23,
    24, 26, 27, 30, 31, 34, 36, 39, 40, 47,
    48, 49, 50, 53, 54, 55, 56, 63, 64, 66,
    74, 81, 85
contracts, 15, 37, 77
control, 7, 9, 29, 37, 44, 52, 69
corn, 49, 52, 64, 84
corporations, 42
correlation, 11
costs, 6, 8, 23, 64, 65, 79
cotton, 8
counsel, 26, 44
counseling, 82
courts, 26, 81
coverage, 28, 29, 37, 48, 49, 53, 54, 56,
    59, 68, 70, 79, 81
covering, 35
credit, 74
crew leaders, 1, 4, 5, 6, 7, 8, 10, 13, 14,
    21, 22, 23, 25, 28, 29, 30, 31, 33, 35,
    49, 53, 54, 55, 58, 59
crime, 16
criticism, 19, 22, 29
crops, 17, 35, 42, 43, 46, 48, 64, 65
cultural, 23
cutters, 49

D

daily living, 75
David Boren, 53
David Stockman, 54, 84
day labor, 54
day-haul operation, 63, 65, 88
death, 70
debeaking, 51, 64
debt, 6
deceit, 1
decisions, 26
deductible, 5
defects, 59
definition, 7, 8, 9, 19, 33, 49, 52, 53, 57,
    60
delivery, 37

Democrat (s), 50, 85
Department of Agriculture, 51
Department of Labor (DOL), 8, 20, 21, 22, 23, 25, 26, 28, 29, 39, 40, 41, 43, 44, 46, 48, 49, 50, 52, 54, 55, 56, 57, 58, 59, 79, 81, 88
Department of State, 48
deported, 47
desire, 9, 83
dichotomy, 69
directives, 19
disability, 27
disabled, 11
disclosure, 70
disenchantment, 34
disputes, 26
dissatisfaction, 58
District of Columbia, 15
division, 23, 62
domestic labor, 12
draft, 30, 81
drinking water, 27
drying, 37
due process, 21
duties, 36, 39, 41, 43

E

earnings, 12, 28
economic, 8, 32, 39, 54, 56
economically disadvantaged, 55
economy, 59, 76
education, 5, 35, 47, 51, 58, 60, 61, 73, 74, 77, 78, 81, 84, 85, 87, 89, 90
elders, 37
election, 86
employees, viii, 8, 12, 35, 36, 37, 41, 43, 44, 50, 51, 52, 54, 55, 56, 57, 59, 64, 87
employers, 23, 26, 28, 30, 31, 33, 40, 47, 56, 57, 58, 60, 63, 68, 69, 74, 76
employment, viii, 1, 6, 7, 11, 12, 14, 15, 16, 17, 19, 23, 32, 34, 37, 38, 46, 48, 55, 57, 59, 62, 63, 64, 65, 66, 84, 88

endangered, 55
English, 22, 23, 31, 46, 50, 65
environment, 1, 50
equipment, 65
equity, 2, 61
evening, 1, 52
evidence, 8, 11, 48, 67
evolution, 2
exclusion, 28
excuse, 67
exercise, 84
exploitation, 20, 59, 61, 74
eyes, 85

F

failure, 21, 40, 57, 61, 69, 74, 81
Fair Labor Standards Act, 80, 81, 90
fairness, 61
false, 16
family, 12, 55, 63, 88
farm (s), vii, 1, 2, 3, 4, 6, 10, 12, 13, 14, 15, 16, 19, 20, 24, 25, 26, 28, 29, 30, 31, 32, 33, 34, 36, 37, 39, 40, 41, 42, 43, 44, 45, 46, 47, 48, 50, 52, 53, 54, 56, 57, 58, 59, 61, 63, 64, 65, 66, 69, 74, 79, 82, 85, 88
farm labor contractor, vii, 3, 4, 13, 14, 15, 16, 19, 20, 25, 29, 30, 31, 32, 37, 41, 42, 43, 44, 45, 46, 54, 56, 63, 64, 65, 66, 69, 79, 82, 88
Farm Labor Contractor Registration Act (FLCRA), vii, viii, 1, 2, 3, 14, 19, 20, 23, 24, 30, 31, 33, 34, 36, 39, 40, 41, 43, 44, 45, 49, 50, 51, 52, 53, 54, 55, 56, 57, 58, 59, 60, 61, 62, 63, 71, 77, 78, 81, 84, 85
farmers, 6, 7, 8, 10, 11, 13, 26, 31, 35, 42, 47, 50, 52, 53, 54, 55, 56, 57, 58, 59, 61, 67, 71, 85, 86
farming, 55
farmworkers, 9, 11, 40, 46, 50, 58, 59, 61, 67, 79
February, 50, 52, 77, 78, 83, 84, 85

federal government, 6, 26
federal law, 68
Federal Register, 19, 77, 82, 83
federalism, 6
fee (s), 4, 8, 14, 27, 44
fiber, 53
film, 1
financial resources, 55
firms, 42, 43, 44
first aid, 28
floating, 12
flow, 14
focusing, 1, 45
food, 4, 53
Ford, 22, 23, 29, 33, 35, 36, 40, 41, 42,
   44, 45, 46, 48, 49, 51, 59, 78, 83
foreign nation, 15
fraud, 32
freedom (s), 51, 52
freezing, 37
Friday, 1
frustration, 69
funds, 79

G

gambling, 4, 6
games, 4
Gaylord Nelson, 20, 58
George Shultz, 20
gloves, 27
good faith, 64
government, 15, 32, 52, 84
grading, 37
grain, 49
grapes, 26
grassroots, 24
groups, 8, 46, 61, 83, 86
growers, 2, 3, 9, 12, 23, 24, 27, 30, 33,
   35, 43, 46, 54, 68, 71, 79
Guam, 15
guest worker, 76
guidance, 43

H

H-2A program, 10
handling, 3, 37, 74
hands, 27, 42, 43
harassment, 53, 58, 59, 61
harmful, 6
Harrison Williams, 3, 24
harvest, 26, 31, 43
harvesting, 43, 46, 49, 50, 51, 63, 64, 65,
   88
hazards, 1
head, 12
health, 28, 37, 50, 51, 55, 77
hearing, 20, 21, 47, 60, 61, 68, 89
heart, 41
high school, 52
hiring, 43, 44, 56, 59, 64
homes, 42, 74
host, 43
House, 3, 10, 13, 14, 20, 33, 34, 35, 36,
   39, 40, 51, 52, 53, 58, 59, 61, 62, 69,
   70, 73, 74, 75, 76, 78, 79, 80, 81, 82,
   83, 84, 85, 87, 89, 90
housing, 4, 9, 12, 17, 26, 37, 42, 49, 59,
   64, 67, 82
Hunting deer, 4
hybrid, 52

I

identification, 15, 32
illegal aliens, 32, 34, 45, 46, 48, 83
imagination, 53
immigration, vii, 2, 13, 16, 31, 32, 34, 83
Immigration and Nationality Act, 88
Immigration Reform and Control Act, 87
implementation, 39, 50, 77
incentive, 24
inclusion, 79
income, 52
indication, 68
industrial, vii

industry, 6, 7, 40, 41, 47, 52, 53, 61, 69, 84

infant mortality rate, 67

injury (ies), 10, 67, 69

innocence, 31

INS, 46, 49

insecurity, 23

inspection (s), 24, 55

inspectors, 24, 28

institutions, 54

insurance, 8, 9, 16, 17, 19, 23, 28, 45, 48, 49, 50, 54, 65

intentions, 53

interpretation, 19, 20, 42, 43, 44, 56, 57, 58

interstate, 6, 9, 14, 15, 19, 22, 29, 30, 37, 45, 48, 63, 79

interstate commerce, 9, 14, 37, 45

intervention, 6

intrastate, 22, 30, 37, 48, 79

investigative, 23

investment, 25

J

Jacob Javits, 3

James Hodgson, 20

James Roosevelt, 3, 74

January, 21, 62, 77, 87

jobs, 11, 32, 34

John Dunlop, 39

John McFall, 39, 85, 41, 42, 53

judge, 7, 26, 32

jurisdiction (s), 26, 37, 58, 66, 69, 78

jury, 7

Justice Department, 21

justification, 7, 16

K

Kenneth Keating, 3

Kentucky, 48

L

labor, vii, viii, 2, 3, 4, 5, 6, 7, 8, 9, 10, 11, 12, 13, 14, 15, 16, 19, 20, 23, 24, 25, 26, 29, 30, 31, 32, 33, 34, 35, 36, 37, 39, 40, 41, 42, 43, 44, 45, 46, 47, 48, 49, 50, 53, 54, 55, 56, 57, 59, 63, 64, 65, 66, 69, 74, 77, 79, 81, 82, 85, 88

language, 23, 24, 34, 41, 42, 47, 50, 59, 65, 68, 80, 87

large-scale, 11, 26

law (s0, 1, 6, 13, 16, 21, 22, 25, 26, 27, 29, 30, 31, 32, 33, 36, 40, 41, 45, 48, 49, 51, 52, 53, 54, 55, 56, 58, 59, 60, 61, 62, 67, 68, 70, 77, 82, 83, 85

lawsuits, 58

lawyers, 46, 48, 50

lead, 9, 53

leadership, 6, 24, 35

legislation, vii, viii, 1, 3, 5, 6, 7, 9, 10, 13, 14, 19, 20, 24, 26, 29, 40, 48, 49, 50, 53, 54, 57, 58, 59, 61, 68, 69, 70, 71, 79, 85, 87

legislative, 25, 31, 50, 52, 61, 83

lettuce, 26

licensing, 6, 8

linguistic, 46, 88

liquor, 6

literacy, 14

litigation, 42, 44, 61, 81, 82

livestock, 65

living conditions, 67

local government, 6

location, 9, 42

M

machinery, 25, 65

malpractice, 6

management, vii, 4, 12, 26, 47, 55, 82

mandates, 14

manpower, 22, 29

marginally skilled, vii
market, 7, 44
Marshall, 52, 53, 55, 56, 57, 59, 84, 85,
    86
Matt Triggs, 5
meals, 82
meanings, 44, 57
measures, 13
mechanical, iv, 84
media, 40
men, 4, 12, 23, 27
Mexican, 11, 12, 47, 76
Mexico, 12, 31, 32, 83
migrant (s), vii, 1, 2, 3, 4, 6, 9, 10, 11,
    12, 13, 14, 15, 16, 17, 19, 22, 29, 35,
    36, 37, 39, 41, 42, 49, 50, 52, 54, 55,
    56, 57, 58, 59, 61, 62, 63, 64, 65, 66,
    67, 74, 77, 88
Migrant and Seasonal Agricultural
    Workers' Protection Act (MSPA), vii,
    viii, 1, 2, 63, 67, 68, 69, 70, 71, 87,
    89, 90
migrant workers, 3, 10, 15, 16, 17, 19,
    22, 35, 36, 39, 41, 42, 50, 52, 54, 55,
    61, 64, 65, 67, 74, 77
minimum wage, 27
minority (ies), 61, 62
misinterpretation, 59
misleading, 5, 16
mobility, 6
momentum, 61
money, 4, 12, 25, 27, 30, 52
morning, 46
motion, 19
movement, 6

N

narcotics, 6
nation, 1, 15
national, 67
National Consumers League, 5
National Council of Agricultural
    Employers, 32, 44, 53, 61, 86, 87, 89

National Labor Relations Act, 26
nationality, 13, 16, 31
Native American (s), 55
naturalization, 49
Nebraska, 49
new, vii, viii, 1, 7, 22, 25, 30, 34, 35, 37,
    38, 49, 50, 57, 61, 62, 63, 69, 71
New Jersey, 10, 27
nonenforcement, 20
non-English speaking, 31, 78
non-profit, 44
normal, 51, 65
North America, 6, 12
North Carolina, 46, 53

O

obligation (s), 35, 38
old-fashioned, 13
operator, 3, 12, 15, 30
opposition, 13, 28, 59, 69
Oregon, 5, 13
organization (s), 1, 7, 15, 55, 57, 61, 63,
    87
oversight, 71
ownership, 37, 43, 65

P

Pacific, 35
packaging, 37
parents, 35
partnerships, 42
payroll, 5, 24
penalty (ies), 13, 18, 21, 33, 34, 56, 57,
    83
Pennsylvania, 4, 58, 86
perceptions, vii
permanent resident, 54
permit, 9
Perry Ellsworth, 44, 53, 82, 87
personal, 10, 15, 24, 52
pesticides, 28

phone, 52
plants, 52
play, 85
poor, 69
port of entry, 48
poultry, 49, 51, 64, 65
poverty, 50
power, 7, 29
premiums, 69
preparation, 43
president, 26
prices, 52
priorities, 29
private, 15, 54, 63, 66, 68, 69, 70
private education, 15, 54
procedures, 59
production, 52, 67
profit, 4, 55
profiteering, 4
program, 1, 10, 11, 12, 25, 61, 67, 76, 83
propaganda, 1
property, 10, 65
prosecutor, 7
prostitute, 5
prostitution, 6
protection, 28, 54, 60, 61, 62
protective clothing, 28
public, 1, 15, 22, 29, 35, 38, 54, 57, 63, 66, 69
public education, 35
public policy, 38, 66, 69
public service, 22
Puerto Rico, 15
punitive, 68

R

radio, 22
radius, 37, 52, 53, 63, 85
rain, 28
range, 30
recall, 25, 42, 80
recognition, 14
recordkeeping, 5, 45

recreation, 82
recruiting, 3, 7, 13, 31, 33, 38, 42, 44
regional, 22
regular, vii, 9, 15, 16, 36, 37, 41, 42, 43, 44, 56, 57, 60, 65
regulation (s), 1, 6, 7, 9, 10, 14, 16, 18, 19, 21, 25, 40, 41, 43, 46, 48, 49, 57, 59, 66, 67, 77, 81, 83, 84
relationship, vii, 41, 43, 70, 78
religious, 7
research, 88
resolution, 20, 59
resources, 29, 54, 56
responsibilities, 5, 30, 78
restructuring, 20, 55, 87
risks, 1
rural, 22

S

safety, 37, 50, 55, 65
salary, 44, 52
sales, 6, 43
Salinas Valley, 81
San Joaquin Valley, 39, 53
Sarah Newman, 5
school, 35
scrip, 4
search, 52
seasonal agricultural worker, 63, 66, 88
security, 34, 74
seed, 52, 84, 88
Senate, 4, 13, 14, 20, 24, 33, 34, 35, 36, 50, 51, 58, 61, 62, 70, 73, 74, 75, 76, 78, 79, 80, 84, 85
Senate Subcommittee on Migratory Labor, 4
series, 19, 42, 44, 49, 59, 75
services, vii, 5, 6, 8, 11, 14, 16, 17, 25, 28, 31, 34, 37, 38, 41, 54, 55, 64, 66
shape, 27
sharing, 4
shearing, 49, 50, 63
sheep, 49, 50, 63, 83

Shooting, 4
short period, vii
sign (s), 20, 32
similarity, 50
skilled, vii, 55
sleep, 27
social security, 5, 23, 25, 27, 28, 47, 74, 77
society, 74
sole proprietor, 42
Solicitor, 20, 43, 45, 46
Spanish-speaking, 13, 40
speculation, 40
spelling, viii
sponsor, 3, 59, 87
stages, 26
standards, vii, 20, 21, 29, 37, 50, 56, 60, 62, 65, 68, 77, 87, 89
State Department, 47, 83
statute of limitations, 70
statutes, vii, viii, 1, 2
statutory, 58, 68, 70, 77
stock, 42
storage, 37
strikes, 55
students, 35, 37, 52, 64
subjective, 43
subpoenas, 67
sugar, 8, 13, 76
summer, 52, 70
supervision, 35, 57
supervisors, 83
supplemental, 9, 29
supply, 2, 4, 7, 66
Supreme Court, 67
surplus, 12

T

tactics, 62
taxpayers, 11, 30
teachers, 35
television, 1, 82
territory, 8

testimony, 20, 28, 34, 50, 61, 67, 81, 84, 87
Texas, 30, 42, 47, 50, 82, 87
Thanksgiving, 1
theory, 4
thinking, 42
threat, 9, 12, 38
threatened, 9
threatening, 39
time, vii, viii, 1, 11, 15, 16, 17, 19, 20, 21, 24, 29, 30, 31, 34, 36, 37, 40, 41, 42, 43, 44, 49, 50, 56, 57, 60, 61, 62, 64, 69, 82
title, 51, 65
Title III, 65
training, viii
transactions, 17
transport, 7, 9, 10, 44, 45, 54, 66
transportation, 4, 12, 17, 27, 29, 31, 42, 49, 50, 54, 59, 64, 65, 74, 79, 83
trucks, 27, 45
truism, 68
trusts, 42
turbulent, 25
turnover, 8

U

unemployment, 34
uniform, 12, 41
United States, 1, 11, 13, 15, 16, 31, 32, 42, 47, 48, 55, 64, 66, 76, 87, 88
unskilled, vii, 11
users, 39

V

variation, 64, 87
vegetables, 26
vehicles, 16, 67
Virginia, 7, 9, 49, 51, 73
voice, 13, 14, 33, 34, 35, 36, 38, 62
voting, 14

W

wage rate, 4, 9, 11, 12, 17, 64, 65
Wage/Hour Division, 20, 21, 29, 31, 46,
  77
wages, 11, 26, 27, 32, 34, 76
Washington, 24, 50, 52, 58, 78, 86, 87
water, 28, 48
wear, 32
welfare, 77
wheat, 49
White House, 51
Willard Wirtz, 5
William Batt, 4
William Hefner, 53

wine, 27
Wisconsin, 22, 30
wisdom, 7
witness (es), 5, 12, 21, 22, 31, 40, 41, 42,
  43, 45, 60, 61, 67
women, 27
workers, vii, 1, 2, 3, 4, 5, 6, 7, 8, 9, 10,
  11, 12, 13, 14, 15, 20, 23, 24, 25, 26,
  27, 28, 29, 30, 31, 32, 33, 36, 37, 40,
  42, 44, 45, 48, 49, 50, 53, 54, 55, 56,
  57, 58, 59, 61, 62, 63, 64, 65, 67, 68,
  69, 70, 74, 76, 77, 82, 84
workforce, vii, 13, 34
working conditions, 9, 11, 32, 76
working hours, 51
writing, 10, 65